To Pauline

Into The Unknown –
Or Is It?

Passages of Discovery

With very best wishes

Elsie Oakensen

By the same Author

One Step Beyond

Into The Unknown – Or Is It?

Passages of Discovery

by

Elsie Oakensen

Regency Press (London & New York) Ltd.
Chaucer House, Chaucer Business Park,
Kemsing, Sevenoaks, Kent TN15 6PW

ISBN 0 7212 0996 3

Printed and bound in Great Britain by
Buckland Press Ltd., Dover, Kent.

CONTENTS

SPREADING THE KNOWLEDGE

ACKNOWLEDGEMENTS

I would like to acknowledge the help and support I have received whilst writing this book, and send grateful thanks to:

My husband JOHN, OUR 3 SONS AND THEIR FAMILIES for their continued support as each new interest in me became apparent, thus prompting them to say, "You've become interested in some very strange things just lately!"

GEORGINA LAURIE who saw what I saw 'on that day' (See Appendix 2) and has typed the contents of this book for me, so leading to a greater understanding for us both of all we have shared in the past – and still do. Also to her husband BRUCE who, like mine, shares our interests and keeps our feet firmly on the ground.

The late KEN PHILLIPS and every UFO Close Encounter Witness I have met over the last 20 years, whose assurances as we travel along our intended pathways, have given to me the knowledge that none of us is ever alone; and to JAMES MILLEN who continued our magazine RAPPORT, thus keeping us all in touch with each other as time passes (p. 14).

CHARLES CHAPMAN, MARY EARP and PETER MACEACHRANE for their encouragement and guidance as an awareness of a Spiritual influence became obvious in my way of life, leading through Healing to my development as a Medium and later to writings, poems and drawings as well as an understanding of life outside the one we know on this planet.

My friend JOAN PEARSON for her friendship and understanding as the years go by.

Elsie Oakensen

DEDICATIONS

This book is dedicated to the memory of the late KEN PHILLIPS and to GEORGINA LAURIE, the two people who came into my life in the most unexpected circumstances and who were each to play a most important part in everything that followed that UFO Close Encounter in 1978. (See Appendix 1)

KEN PHILLIPS

Ken Phillips, BEd., BA., was a mathematician and anthropologist who had been with The British UFO Research Association (BUFORA) for many years as an Investigator and Researcher, and latterly was also the Editor of their magazine UFO TIMES.

With Dr Alex Keul from Salzburg University he developed the Anamnesis Protocol which detailed the recollections of those of us involved in UFO Close Encounters. This was all done within a disciplined, scientific framework.

Since 1983 he was England's leader in this Research which showed the witnesses to be perfectly normal people and in many cases to have an above average intelligence, with a heightened Extra Sensory Perception level. This fact stood out sharply within this many-faceted research, also in a comparative analysis with control groups.

Ken was my first contact with BUFORA in 1978 when I drove under my UFO and it was a letter from him in February 1990 which invited me to join a number of other Close Encounter Witnesses at a meeting in London from which the UFO WITNESS SUPPORT GROUP (WSG) was formed.

He was the rock on which this group was founded and felt very strongly that a network of understanding should be formed throughout the United Kingdom so that witnesses everywhere would know that there was always someone somewhere – perhaps only a telephone call away – who would listen and understand.

There was also an opportunity to meet at regular intervals at the WSG meetings which were arranged mostly in London but also in other parts of the country, and there was contact for us all through our Magazine RAPPORT which was Ken's idea and to which we all contributed. But most important was the personal contact available from Ken who was never too busy to talk to us on the phone. We were all touched by his integrity and sincerity.

Ken was a very well-read man with a remarkable memory, who could readily draw from this fund of knowledge a relevant example of a similar experience to that being discussed, so furthering the discussion and leading it into other aspects of the phenomenon. He had that special kind of understanding which UFO Close Encounter Witnesses need and which is so rarely found in someone outside the UFO experience. We trusted him implicitly.

After our encounters, as we began to notice our lives going into unpredictable areas, Ken's support was readily available. He knew us all personally and new members could always be linked up with someone from within their own category residing within their own area of the UK. Ken's mind was open to all eventualities; his listening skills and ability to sum up the situation were second to none.

Because of this unique understanding and rapport which he had with us all, he is very sadly missed and no one else can possibly understand the affection we all felt for him and his wife Anne, who fully supported Ken's work with us. She provided refreshments after our long journeys to the meetings and welcomed us into their home when we viewed a relevant video. We were all made to feel like their extended family.

Thanks to his devotion the Witness Support Group continues to this day and his memory has been honoured by adding his name to the title. Members of the KEN PHILLIPS WITNESS SUPPORT GROUP who are unable to attend meetings still keep in touch with each other through RAPPORT, the magazine he initiated, and as time passes so our membership numbers increase.

We have all endeavoured to keep alive all that he did for the benefit of UFO Close Encounter Witnesses everywhere. He lives on in our hearts and I for one will never forget the guidance and support which I received from him as I have travelled along the pathways which I describe in this book.

Thank you Ken. God Bless You.

THE WITNESS SUPPORT GROUP
Where do we go from here?

I'm at Northampton station
To travel on a train,
A different destination
This time to attain.

A meeting held in London
I'm heading for today,
To breathe new life into the group
And help it on its way.

Without Ken we must go on
To further the aims he set,
Leading us forward into new fields
With wonder – not regret.

Different facets of knowledge
In this wondrous development,
At previous meetings we've discussed.
A time we felt well–spent.

We found we'd gelled into a group
Where understanding grew.
Openness and honesty played their part,
Confidentiality too.

Although our experiences differed
(No two were exactly the same)
The legacies we noticed later
Were similar. A real gain

Towards a complete understanding
Of where we fitted in,
And the part we would finally play
When supposition came to an end.

Sadly the hopes that the UFO Witness Support Group should continue after that meeting failed to materialise and BUFORA closed down the group soon afterwards.

Then, like the Phoenix it rose again in an unexpected way. Ken Phillip's magazine RAPPORT was continued under the Editorship of James Millen and it now flourishes – being funded, written and distributed entirely by the Witnesses themselves and linking together witnesses in all parts of the United Kingdom.

Elsie Oakensen

SOUL MATES?

My first contact with Jenny Randles was in her role as BUFORA's Director of Investigations.

In the 1970s not many UFO encounters involving a time-loss were being reported so my experience aroused great interest within the Association. Also, I guess, a certain amount of frustration, because the people who it was felt could corroborate it had requested confidentiality and that had to be respected.

However this subject did arise on the odd occasion as it was important in as much that the tightening sensation around my head in the evening seemed to coincide with the strange experience witnessed by those other people about four miles away from where I was at that time. (Appendix 2.)

Jenny was always certain that one day we would meet. "And when you do," she would emphasise, "I wouldn't mind betting that you and the driver of that car, Georgina Laurie, will find that you have an awful lot in common." I was not so sure.

But many years later that contact really was made and caused great excitement in our area. The Daventry Express awarded it the honour of a front page report, which resulted in later editions carrying further reports of sightings on that same night including corroboration of Georgina's report by one of the passengers in her car.

What has followed since is recorded in our own words.

ELSIE'S STORY

Have you ever spoken to a complete stranger and felt that you have known that person all your life? Well that's exactly how I felt when Georgina Laurie phoned me.

In 1978 when I drove under my UFO I had a time loss and later realised that, not only the light at that time of day, but time itself, my car and I were all manipulated by some kind of external force or energy, or perhaps 'beings'.

After the BUFORA investigation I was told that about two hours later four ladies had been travelling in a car from their homes in the village of Byfield to a WI meeting at Preston Capes a few miles away and that they'd had a strange experience also; the assumption being that 'my' UFO was still in the area at that later time.

I knew the names of these ladies but also understood that they did not want to contact me, nor to take the matter further. Because confidentiality is an important part of Ufology where witnesses are concerned, I respected that decision, and over the years I had never made any attempt to contact them, nor did any of them contact me – but the surname of the driver of that car did ring a bell at the time.Almost 17 years to the day after the event I had picked up my telephone and heard a lady's voice telling me that she was Georgina Laurie.

"I saw what you saw on that day," were her next words and I listened to her voice telling me something I already knew about, which the UFO world had said over the years had corroborated that which had happened to me on that same day – but for reasons best known to each of us, neither had ever made contact with the other during that time.

On this particular day she had read an article about me in the Northampton Chronicle & Echo newspaper which reported the UFO sighting, my development as a Healer and the fact that my book ONE STEP BEYOND had been published.

As she talked I felt as if I was looking into a mirror and was seeing my own reflection talking back to me – but actually I was listening on the telephone to a stranger's voice relating my thoughts and describing the happenings in my own life. It was as if it was actually me talking and repeating these things which I already knew – to myself.

"We've known about you all along," she said, "but Bruce said that now you are a Healer and so am I, I really should get in touch." Bruce? That rang a bell too.

When I left College in 1948 my first teaching post had been in Byfield School, and during each week in term time I had lodged in a house which I learned was next door to the one in which Bruce and his family had lived. Also during that time he was actually a pupil in the school.

Georgina (Georgie) and I are now members of the National Federation of Spiritual Healers and during the previous 12 months had both received Healing Certificates for First and Second Degree REIKI.

We are both finding that we have an ability to draw and we both use a pendulum and share an interest in crystals.

Bruce and I are writing poetry whilst Georgina and my husband John, are both Parish Clerks. Each family has 3 sons and no daughters and the youngest son in each family lives in Weedon and the oldest child of each is a girl, whilst Georgina and I now find ourselves living in adjacent villages separated by the section of the A5 along which my UFO encounter took place.

As we spoke the term 'SOUL MATE' came into my mind. Over the years the possibility of contact was mentioned several times by Jenny Randles who has always maintained that if Georgina and I ever did meet we would find that we had an awful lot in common. This has now been proved to be very accurate.

Since then the two of us were invited to recount our experiences for a reconstruction to be included in a programme which was shown on ITV in Autumn 1996.

Nothing related here could possibly have been envisaged on 22nd November 1978 but amazingly it has all come about since that time.

The title of the TV Series? Oh yes – STRANGE BUT TRUE – ENCOUNTERS? – What else could it have been!

Elsie Oakensen 1998

GEORGINA'S STORY

As I typed this book for Elsie I could hardly believe my eyes for in every section what had happened to Elsie had either happened or was happening to me. From the sighting of the UFO right through to the here and now. The coincidences we have shared both married with three sons and more.

Healing – I too was told I would come to mediumship through healing and that for me healing would no longer be a set thing just perhaps a touch or smile.

Jacqueline, an eleven year old girl in Spirit, is just communicating through me.

I too had done drawings although I cannot draw.

I had written poems which too I normally cannot do.

I had even touched on psychometry.

When my Healing Circle finished, I started up my own only to find it was to develop mediumship to all who are in that group.

For me it was a Tarot reading that set me on my path. I was told I was a Healer and would sit in a development circle. This too I didn't understand and had to find out. Eventually I ended up in a development circle. A friend had been trying to persuade me to have my cards read for 7 years until one day out of the blue I decided this was what I wanted to do.

A lot of questions and the answers too I found as I sat and typed those pages. As I read her first book 'One Step Beyond' I couldn't believe what I saw. Things that had been happening to me had happened to Elsie too.

Georgina Laurie 1998

IT ALL STARTED LIKE THIS

"I've been there, done that,"
I said the other day.
"And I've got the T-shirt."
What else can I say.

My car had malfunctioned
And daylight disappeared.
Circles of brilliant white light have
On the road appeared.

They had no beams, so from above
They certainly must have come,
But I could see nothing there at all
As I journeyed home.

Then later than expected
I arrived home that day,
Wondering what it was that I
Drove under on the way.

"Oh, it's a UFO," they said.
It was most very strange.
Did anyone else see it,
Or was it out of range?

But Georgie and her friends
Later were driving along
When their car was affected too
By strange things going on.

The red and green lights I had seen,
They could see them too.
They paced their car along the road
And interest in them grew.

But they knew not what they had seen
As nor indeed did I,
But none-the-less it was something strange
That day in the darkening sky.

Elsie Oakensen

INTO THE UNKNOWN

AUTHOR'S INTRODUCTION

THE UFO PHENOMENON

'Each Close Encounter which witnesses have is only the beginning of a wonderful new experience.

It is the awakening of a new understanding which, as time passes, grows into an awareness of a new and previously unknown way of life, or existence, outside the one with which you are familiar. An existence in a new dimension out in the vast area of space which fills the universe. An area where souls can grow and develop a greater awareness of all that is to be.

Your planet earth is nearing depletion now. Man is destroying what he has been given because of greed and lack of concern for others. The earth's energy needs to be renewed and revitalised for man's continued existence there. This will happen, but the lives of the chosen ones will continue further into the future when this has been accomplished.

Until then conditions will become exaggerated in strength. The weather patterns will be as never before and the earth itself will become unrecognisable. Our ships are ready to accommodate all those who have proven their worth to inhabit the new earth and to live with He who will return.

The master plan is ready. Do not let it worry you. You and your family will experience wonders you have not experienced before and which you would never believe possible.

Spread love everywhere. Positive thoughts help too. Go forward and do not hesitate. All will be well.'

THE UFO PHENOMENON HAS MANY FACETS.
THIS IS THE STORY OF ONE OF THEM – THE ONE
IN WHICH I INADVERTENTLY BECAME INVOLVED.

After the hypnosis session following my UFO encounter I was advised to read no books about UFOs so that my mind was clear regarding my own experience as I tried to understand the implications of it. Over the time since then I have found that to have been excellent advice.

Now I have applied the same principle to my work for, and my understanding of Spirit. I have felt that I would be guided along whichever pathway was the right one for me by my Guides and Helpers, and as I write this book I know it will be about my own 'discoveries' and will not be influenced by the works and experiences of others.

Sixteen years after my UFO experience the Spirit World made contact in a way I could never have imagined at the time.

AWARENESS OF SPIRIT

'You are finding now as you speak to UFO witnesses that the Spiritual aspects of life are commonplace in discussion among you. A much greater awareness of Spirit is blossoming now, an understanding of which you are all becoming aware.

But much more love than is given at present is required to heal the earth planet and raise it to a higher vibration within the universe, the transition is very slow. The time is short for all that is necessary to be done to complete this operation.

A new awareness is coming, but very slowly for some who will not be ready to receive our news of the final happening before a brand new beginning.

To include many of our messages to you in your book will help the readers to understand all that is to come.

We will be with you as you write and help you to select the appropriate passage to include. You will get great satisfaction from doing this and together we shall tell the world the meaning of all things which appear as a mystery to them at present.

Their eyes will be opened and they will see the light.

Their ears will hear the trumpets declaring the coming of the Great One.

Their hearts will be ready to accept the true love of the Master. A very happy future awaits.'

Elsie Oakensen

A PROMISE TO MYSELF

One of my earliest memories of St. Nicholas's Church in Potterspury was a thought-provoking prediction which had made a great impression on my young mind during a Sunday School Class.

I don't remember the Sunday School teacher or precisely where our young class sat within the building itself but on that day the word SOUL had been mentioned and I learned that I had got one – in fact that each of us there had one.

On our return home from anywhere we had visited in those early days of our lives, my brother Ted and I were always encouraged to tell our parents what had happened.

On that particular Sunday I was excited and was asked, "Why?" I was about six years old and went on to explain that when we died this soul left our bodies and went to Heaven.

At this point Mum explained to us a little about death. I remember her saying that as she was older than we were we could expect that she would die before we did. She noticed our concern.

"You mustn't worry," she said, "I shall be in Heaven. It is a lovely place with big gardens and lots of beautiful flowers." Then she added, "You must not be sad when I go because I shall be very happy there and you must be happy for me," and we promised that we would.

Not long afterwards I had some more news to relay after Sunday School. Jesus had died on a cross and his soul had gone to Heaven – but HE was coming back.

For some reason which I did not understand at the time, that piece of news was so exciting that I needed to know more. "When?" I had asked expectantly, but my hopes were shattered as no one seemed to have an answer. Then, like a flash a voice in my head said, 'The year 2000.'

In the 1930s that was a long way off and I hoped and prayed that I would live long enough to witness the scene, but nobody knew where or exactly when it would be.

After Sunday School on that day the most important task was to find how old I would be in the year 2000. These were big numbers for a small girl to handle and Dad suggested that I wrote down 2000, then underneath it I wrote the year of my birth 1928. He said that if we took one from the other I would then know how old I would be at that time.

With his help we arrived at the answer: 72. I remember thinking that was as old as my Grandmother. It was a long way to go, but I would do my best to still be around when Jesus came back to the earth.

That was a promise I made to myself on that day all those years ago and, because of the events described in this book I know I shall keep it.

UFOs – WHAT ARE THEY?

'For some time now the importance of the witnesses has been lost as those who try to find answers lose sight of the importance of those who will be able to supply them.'

SOLVING THE PUZZLE

"What's a UFO?" I asked the young man who had volunteered this information after I had described my Close Encounter to a group at the Teachers' Centre.

"An Unidentified Flying Object," he had replied. Very true, but not very helpful!

I now believe that when I had what the British UFO Research Association (BUFORA) categorised as a Close Encounter of the Fourth Kind – an Alien Abduction Experience – it could have been my first contact with the Spirit World.

On that day as I drove along the A5 at Weedon in Northamptonshire this dumb-bell shaped object was immediately above the road in front of me and I, with many other vehicles drove directly underneath it.

After that my car electrics malfunctioned, natural daylight disappeared completely and as I sat in that blackness, circles of brilliant white light about a metre in diameter, and with no beams at all, shone on to the ground one at a time in a semicircular pattern around the front of the car punctuating the blackness and showing me that my car had travelled about 100 yards around a right-angled bend in the road without me knowingly being in control of it.

Then to add to the intrigue, when I arrived home I found that my journey had taken twice as long as it usually did.

About twelve years later I saw a spectacular display of lights in a cloud-covered sky in the same area. These changed shape five times in five minutes as I watched and the paranormal experiences which followed caused my life to completely change direction. (Appendix 3.)

Gradually a deeper understanding of a Spiritual involvement was becoming apparent to me. New information via a variety of sources was coming my way, and there was this entirely new meaning and direction in my way of life.

Casting my mind back to that day when I'd had that initial contact with something outside my normal human understanding, my life had begun to function on a completely different ‘wavelength’. No longer was contact with human beings the be-all and end-all of life on this planet, I had entered into a completely new dimension of understanding which was daily becoming more comprehensible to me.

Human contacts made over the years were beginning to fall into different categories and were either still giving to me the most loyal support I could ever have expected, or had travelled a short distance with me, then fallen by the wayside. But each one, no matter how short the relationship, played an important part in the unfoldment towards that final awareness of what the future was to hold.

Some of these contacts had been attending exotic courses, studying subjects I didn’t understand; subjects obviously relevant to their own spiritual development but seemingly not absolutely essential to my own.

In my case, at that point SIMPLICITY became the watchword.

Although I’d had regular contact with BUFORA officials during those years since my sighting and I’d heard names of other witnesses there was never any suggestion that we should actually meet and I began to wonder whether we were intentionally being kept apart.

I am a great believer that if something is meant to be then it will happen anyway, and looking back it now seems that my part in all that has happened – and is yet to come – was meant to be going on all around me and to become a personal learning experience in stages of understanding at my own level, and on a time scale which would bring me to the required level of achievement for any purpose which would be required of me in the future.

The first thing I had learned from Graham Allen, the first person I ever met who had also had a UFO Close Encounter of the Fourth Kind, was that we each had a part to play in the final plan for a perfect world and that each one’s part would be different.

He likened it to a jigsaw puzzle where no two pieces are exactly the same and it takes all the pieces together to form a complete picture. Each of us would be trained in our own special way, and at the end when we all meet, each one’s efforts will slot together perfectly. The final pattern will be complete and each one’s contribution will have been equally important towards the completion of the whole.

Each may seem similar perhaps in shape or design, but along the way each person will receive specialist help and advice in the form of memories from previous reincarnations, not only on planet earth but on other planets, in other times and dimensions out there in space – a wondrous miscellany of experiences towards soul-growth – and each soul having a different pattern within that growth.

It was Graham’s analogy of the ‘pieces of a jigsaw puzzle’ which has surfaced many times over the years that have followed, especially in my travels, as I met people who seemed to stay awhile and then pass on to pastures new, realising later that we obviously, at that time needed to pass to each other a piece of information which at that point we could share, and by doing so we would be enriching that which we were collecting on our journeys to our final destinations.

Sometimes after such encounters I would feel drained. "You'll feel better now he/she's gone off your pathway," I was told. "Some people are givers, some are takers, and that one was a taker."

But even so, when I have looked back and summed up the episode, there has always been something positive which has come from it. Sometimes it is easier to sweep this kind of thing under the carpet and pretend it never happened, particularly if at that time you feel hurt by what has occurred.

But as time passed I realised that something very important was actually happening during these times, and that these experiences had occurred for a reason – to bring me down to earth with a bump – and there was my answer, which was followed by a spiritual message.

'Sometimes in this life when we become complacent, there has to be a setback or two to give us the opportunity to reassess the ways in which we need to go forward.

It gives us time to assess the situation, to analyse all points of reference which have arisen, and to regain confidence in our own abilities to organise ourselves, and dead wood can be cleared away so that our work can go forward more smoothly and with greater purpose.'

I now understood myself better and I add another spiritual thought for good measure.

'EVERY NEGATIVE ACTION IS A LEARNING EXPERIENCE.'

Then all of these blend together to become a wonderful assortment of true and balanced learning experiences which play a large part in the shaping of our future lives.

Another reassuring message was to follow –

'You know that you can reach us whenever you need us. WE ARE ONLY A THOUGHT AWAY and we shall always be there for you.

Do not worry about others. You are going along different pathways at present, but you will all reach the end of your journeys at the same place and at the same time.

The final destination is for all, but each of you has a completely different set of achievements to accomplish to enable you to be proficient in the part that destiny has prepared for you to play.

We are guiding you in the correct direction along which you will find many challenges to overcome. These you will do well because of the training we are giving you.'

SPECULATION ABOUT UFOs

Concern that the inhabitants of the earth are not listening to the witnesses, regarding the reasons for UFO sightings, was expressed by Spirit and to clarify this point I have used examples from my own experience to illustrate the situation.

'There is much speculation in your world about that which you call UFOs,' Spirit writes. 'Many people are trying to find an explanation. They all need to know. If only they would get together and talk to each other instead of vie-ing with each other to be the first one at the winning-post.

Each one has an element of truth in his understanding but is blinkered because he is concerned that someone else might reach the winning-post first.'

HOW TRUE.

This is something of which the UFO witnesses have been aware during this decade at least. As new books and magazines on the subject have been published the audacity and thoughtlessness of some authors and journalists have caused much distress to those whose names and addresses have been published and those whose accounts, sometimes with very intimate details were used. In others witnesses were not given the opportunity of an interview or the courtesy of being asked to proofread an account before publication.

During these years I found myself also in this category and the UFO Witness Support Group meetings certainly lived up to their name. Those of us who attended felt in great need of support from each other. We each understood fully how the others felt. Amongst most there was a total feeling of helplessness in not being able to correct these dreadful inaccuracies. Some had also by then been deprived of the confidentiality which was promised to them when the initial investigation had taken place.

We had all been on the receiving end of public ridicule when first admitting to a strange encounter and now here was more – only this was much worse and some seemed to come about intentionally.

Those with pet theories concerning a reason for UFOs seemed to change our facts to fit their theories. Others gave no thought at all to the damage being done by them to the witnesses' credibility when the accurate details given by that witness in an interview were distorted and twisted in the published accounts.

They could not possibly understand the inner knowledge which we were given at the time of our encounters – and many never tried to understand.

During this time John Spencer, who is at past Chairman of BUFORA, suggested that more could possibly be known about the UFO phenomenon if the witnesses carried out an investigation into their own sightings. This he described as Witness-Driven Investigation.

As time passed I felt the need to know more about what had happened to me – and especially why I had been chosen for that experience. So in my retirement that exercise became my main aim. It was completed to my own satisfaction and the details were published by Regency Press in 1996 entitled ONE STEP BEYOND – A Personal UFO Abduction Experience.

Then sadly, those with closed minds refused to accept that a UFO CE4* experience could be a Spiritual one, even though many other witnesses had, by then, come to the same conclusion. So once again there were derisory remarks to contend with.

Ridicule to me is a negative thing but I also believe that negative acts are learning experiences. One message of encouragement I have received from Spirit reads:–

'A positive attitude to all things smoothes out what could be a very stony pathway and life will be so much easier to bear.'

So I set about collecting all the ridiculous things said and written about me and my UFO experience during those years and, after small truthful explanations are added, what were previously looks of horror on people's faces when they first heard have now become very broad grins, and during serious conversations, lectures and talks this now forms an oasis of light relief.

[The full truthful version of my Close Encounter can be read in Appendix 1 and comparisons can then be made with the following.]

Over the years I have been told, or have read these things which have been made public about me and my sighting.

- As brilliant white lights flashed on the road at the front of the car she 'saw aliens around the UFO.' I did not.
- I had been rejected by these aliens because 'I was past child-bearing age' – which I wasn't. I was 49 – but then nobody consulted me about that!
- I had said that I 'was promised a return visit.' I hadn't.
- I was the Head of the 'Daventry Teacher Training Centre.' No such place exists.
- The dumb-bell shaped object 'spanned the entire width of the dual-carriageway' – which isn't even there.
- I was married to a 'Police Chief Inspector'. John said that promotion would have been much more appreciated if it had come 16 years earlier when he was actually in the Police Force.

* Close Encounter of the 4th Kind – a UFO Abduction experience.

- It would seem that I 'could not recall seeing any other traffic on that section of the A5 on that day'. It was a very busy trunk road and I could only travel at the same speed as the rest of the vehicles going in the same direction.
- 'The circles of light danced around her car in an almost choreographed routine'. – Rubbish!
- 'Her head was whirling'. It wasn't.
- I was 'stranded in a broken-down car' – one which started up by itself and has driven normally ever since.
- In one book my hypnosis session was written as if I was actually speaking myself. I queried this with the author. He said he used the transcript from my hypnosis session which he had got from my BUFORA Case-file. I asked how he had managed to gain access to my Case-file as he was a free-lance journalist and he named the BUFORA official who had allowed him to use it.

  I had questioned the way it was written because I knew that there never had been a transcript of my hypnosis session. Nothing was ever found to be useable on the tapes supposedly recording the session, and the only records of it are those notes which I wrote myself afterwards, from memories which came during the following weeks. These were written, signed and dated by me at the time and legally are my copyright – but no one asked my permission to use them.

  At the end of this account, inaccurate though it was, it was pointed out to the reader that I was 'undoubtedly a credible witness'. Those magic words seem to impress the Media but they did not impress me. I was the ONLY witness and no one outside that experience is in any way qualified to make any judgement regarding that aspect of any witness's character.
- Another author emphasised that he was going to write about me in a book he planned. I suggested we should arrange a time for an interview, but he insisted that there was no need to interview me as he was going to copy another author's version of my story from that already published book – and nothing I said would convince him of the importance of interviewing the actual witness whom he even planned to name.

  I was told, in no uncertain terms, that my experience had happened so long ago and that it had been written about so often that no one was interested in it anyway.

  I replied by asking – "If this is your opinion of my story why have you resurrected this old-fashioned, over-exposed account to use in a book written by you?" I am still waiting for a satisfactory reply! Whether he mentioned me or not I don't know. He never had the courtesy to send me a copy.
- Then we also come up against people with their own theories about UFOs. There is nothing wrong with that, except that their main aim seems to be to prove that our experiences can be easily explained away by some scientific reasoning, and that by blinding us with science they can convince us that nothing ever happened to us.

If you have seen a UFO beware of the person who uses the word 'hallucinated'. I have had two experiences of this.

- The first gentleman refused to talk to me but he did write. It seemed that he felt an urgency to speak to my husband so that he could set his (my husband's) mind at rest. He wanted John to know that on the day of my sighting I had a visual seizure on my way home from work and had hallucinated. And this was while I was in control of a car on a very busy trunk road. Now when you consider that the said gentleman had never discussed my sighting with me but was prepared to come out of the blue to tell my husband of 45 years something about his wife which neither of us knew, and which my doctor had never diagnosed, this was a very brave act on his part, especially as he had no medical qualifications to equip him to diagnose any medical condition whatever.

  This intrusion into our privacy was something new at that time and I couldn't help visualising the situation if the two had actually met. It would have been a meeting of a small, assertive man with a very much larger, very placid one, and every time I think of it I see (size-wise) Laurel and Hardy, with John patting him on the head and saying, "There, there. Never mind!"
- The second gentleman knows a great deal more about astrology than I am ever likely to know, but has read ONE STEP BEYOND and is now applying that science to my sighting.

He claims that as I drove home on that evening (22nd November 1978) I was looking in a SE or a SSE-ly direction and 'the object she saw could have been a mirage of a first magnitude star. Fomalhaut was setting in the SSE and at 17.30 hrs (for example) was on a bearing of 161° at an altitude of only 60°. Such a mirage can have been caused by a temperature inversion.' (UFO TIMES – Issue 41. May/June p.19)

My own knowledge of mirages is very simple and dates back to my schooldays during World War 2 when I learned that mirages were associated with travellers in the desert who, when dying of thirst, would possibly see an oasis which wasn't actually there.

He seems to associate the tightening sensations around my head, several hours before and after the sighting as being connected in some way with an hallucination, which I assume is what he refers to as a mirage, BUFORA categorised as a UFO and I still call a dumb-bell shaped object.

On that day as I was driving towards this variably-described object in a south-easterly direction I was given a side view of it.

As it straddled the road, about 50 feet wide and 100 feet above it (BUFORA's estimations) I was compelled to travel with the other traffic underneath it, and looking up I could see the underside of it as I did so.

Continuing my journey still in a south-easterly direction it was behind me. I stopped at the top of the next hill and looked back. It was still there and I then saw the other side of it.

I can accept that if it had been a mirage of that particular star I could have seen it when travelling in a south-easterly direction, but would I have been able to drive UNDER it, and if so, when I later stopped and looked back at it from the other side, then in a north-westerly direction, would I have been able to see it reversed? Because, at that point the star was actually BEHIND me.

If the answer to each of these questions is YES then I must be the only person in the world who has seen a mirage, driven under it, then turned round and seen it from the other side.

You can understand why Spirit has noticed 'much speculation' in this world about that which we call UFOs. The people who formulate these theories delight in telling the witnesses what really happened to them and what it was that they actually saw, even though they were not there themselves at the time. Unfortunately these are the versions the public reads and accepts.

Advice to them from Spirit was forthcoming:–

> 'Slow down. Talk to each other honestly and openly and without malice and it will be as if you all hold one small section of the completed puzzle. Put them together carefully and the solution will become apparent.
>
> Or, easier still, listen to those who know. You cast aside the wise ones, those who have 'been there, done that, got the T-shirt' – a popular saying which is applicable in this case also.
>
> Their understanding comes through experience and there is no better way to learn.'

It is because of these speculations that I have come to realise how different and extra-ordinary my sighting must appear to those who feel that UFOs can be explained away in very simple terms.

The events I described at the beginning of this section are all so very different and each happened at a different point over a 2-mile journey, not whilst standing still and looking up into the sky as most witnesses do. Also during a 6 hour period if you include the tightening sensations around my head which I experienced at lunch time and again after 7 p.m. on that same day.

This is a spectacular variety of happenings – all I expect to indicate to me that this was an occasion, so important that it must be indelibly impressed upon my mind, in order to give me much food for thought over the following years, thus making the importance of these happenings very very clear as I worked during that time to unfold the mystery of it all.

WISE ADVICE – and very apt in my case.

'Do not fear ridicule.
It is the outward manifestation of ignorance.'

THAT INDESCRIBABLE FEELING

One evening as I sat writing, something very profound happened – a wonderful awareness seemed to fill my whole being. It was if a completely new understanding of all that had happened before had come to fruition. I was no longer searching for answers. They were all there before me.

It was a feeling I shall treasure for the rest of my life, and from that day onwards I entered into a new kind of understanding and a very close working relationship with Spirit. It was something so personal to me that I could not explain it. No words seemed adequate to describe it.

About three years after this I sat listening to a speaker recounting an experience which she had. Suddenly I was transfixed. There was an immediate rapport between us. This was something which we had both shared. Here was another UFO witness searching for the appropriate words to use to describe it.

"I don't know how to explain how I felt at that moment," she said, and I knew exactly what she meant. Words had failed me too. They all seemed so inapt.

Mine was such a private experience that I felt unable to tell anyone about it, not even members of my own family, nor my closest friends. I was sure that no one else could possibly understand my feelings at that time. I was not sure that I could understand them myself, and was quite incapable of putting them into words which anyone else would comprehend.

On that day I was experiencing something so completely different from any earthly emotions, so out of this world that I felt I didn't want to share it with anyone.

The speaker to whom I was listening had released those emotions which I had kept hidden for so long and the feeling of being alone completely disappeared. She and I shared something which only we can know – a feeling which unfortunately we cannot describe adequately to someone outside that experience and so enable them to fully understand as well.

My hope is that in the not-too-distant future others will realise that they too have already shared our experience.

UFOs – THE ANSWERS

'WHAT IS A UFO?' I had asked – now I knew.

A UFO is an extra-terrestrial craft which can travel inter-dimensionally through time and space, every now and again visiting the lower dimensions in the Universe, and whilst there it occasionally allows someone on the earth planet to have a glimpse of it and during that time that lucky person is given an inner knowledge and an understanding of life outside the one into which he/she was born.

Then, according to the knowledge which has built up within us through our Spirit's growth over many generations, re-incarnations, and life in other times and other dimensions out there in space, we have an understanding which, despite its growth has lain hidden until now when with this sighting these past earthly and extra-terrestrial memories have been awakened.

Confirmation of this and the reasons for these sightings were to follow.

'You and other witnesses are right to understand that what you have experienced is a Spiritual one and that there is nothing to fear. We are helping you all to save the world from destruction. So much wrong is occurring now that nothing resembles the things you remember as children.

Sadly the behaviour of the earth's inhabitants has changed to such an extent that negative thoughts in some cases outnumber positive ones. Love and understanding of one another's feelings can change things for the better. A positive outlook on life is necessary; a going-forward to promote the good side of all happenings, instead of negative attitudes to so much, will help this awareness to develop.

Go forward. Spread the word by example and understanding will grow – and love to all men will have an abundance of worthwhile effect on the outcome of all that will be in the future'.

THE VALUE OF THE WITNESS

In August 1996 I received information that my contact with Spirit through UFOs was enormously valuable for mankind in general and that I am one of a small, but growing group of people whose job it is to awaken extra-terrestrial memories of humans at a time when there is an enormous transition occurring – a shift from fear into Love, and an alignment of humanity to a greater truth and a greater Light.

I am here at this time to participate with others, who have also experienced UFO encounters (during which time we were personally awakened) in passing on the information we have received and all that will be coming to us in the future.

We shall find that many, many people are on the edge of remembering. Many more are wanting to remember. Others are vaguely interested and the rest don't care either way. It is best that our energies should be utilised to the maximum effect through honesty and blatant truth in the appropriate situation and with discernment and selective information in other situations.

This I was told will be the most important task in our lives. It is what we were born to do and we are advised to take heart from the extra-terrestrials awaking around us so that humanity can release itself to a greater perspective.

WITNESS GUIDANCE
(including Spiritual Writings)

'We shall need your help. We shall show you the way you can serve us best. You will play an important part in preaching the truth to many who do not understand.

Our messages to mankind will be coming to you all in a very positive way. They will be simple and easily understood. We shall speak to many like you who have been contacted before. You will all understand and will all be given the opportunities necessary to disseminate the information. World-wide we shall make contact. You will not be alone.

You will all speak as with one tongue and will all be understood.

We are preparing the way for the Lord, the Great Messiah, the King of Peace.

Be ready and speak only the TRUTH which we shall give you, and which will be heard by many.'

CALMNESS

'As time passes you will develop qualities of wisdom, healing and spiritual peace. You have already started on this road and the changes will begin to become noticeable in you, by others close to you, very soon.

You will have a form of serenity denoting calmness, and a balance of understanding which you have long admired in others you have met along life's pathway. You remember the Woodwork Master who always put another point of view to anyone who was upset.

Sometimes under these conditions you can only see one point of view and it needs another to get things into perspective. You are now going forward in this way and will be able to calm others when necessary, remembering the help you have received yourself in the past.

Go ahead in this way and help others to turn negative attitudes into positive and beneficial blessings.'

TRAINING

'You are all being trained by us to be able to spread the word – each in your own way, differently yet very similarly. You each have a style which is very right for you. This training comes in your sleep. The methods to use and the information to give is being made known to you.

You will find this work rewarding and many will hear the word and know that the time is near for the transformation and cleansing of the earth. The people's level of consciousness will be raised.

The evacuation of the earth will be accomplished satisfactorily. You all have a place where you will grow in spiritual awareness and come face-to-face with the Master.

Work well. The pathway is long and smooth, exciting and very rewarding. You will meet very interesting people along the way and benefit from their kind of knowledge too.

We watch over you. guide you and guard you. We will enfold you and keep you safe.'

When I received the next message it came as a surprise. Looking back I seem to have always taken life and the jobs I have done during it for granted, as a normal progression in what I was doing at the time to further my qualifications in that particular area.

In 1976 I completed a course for a Diploma in the Teaching of Reading at Leicester University so it seemed logical then to change my post as the Deputy Head of Braunston Church of England School and look for something different.

A Teachers' Centre had opened in Daventry a year or so before this and the person in charge had just been appointed to a new school where she was to take up the post of Head Mistress. I stepped in to cover until the post was advertised and later when this happened I applied for it and was appointed on a permanent basis.

My main task there was to be in close contact with the surrounding schools, to learn their requirements for the In-Service Training of their staff and to organise the Courses which would supply their needs. With close co-operation from the Education Authority's Inspectorate provision was made and subsequently relevant courses were organised from my Centre.

I never lectured at any myself. Those who did so were experts in their subjects and could provide the teachers attending with the most detailed and up-to-date information. I remained in that post for eight years until I was forced to retire through ill-health and it was a very interesting and rewarding ending to my teaching career.

This message from Spirit made me realise that life itself is a learning experience in preparation for a greater understanding towards the soul's growth.

CONFIRMATION AND ENCOURAGEMENT

'Tonight our message to you is to keep travelling along the way you are going. All you hope to learn will come your way when you least expect it. Do not push it. When the time is right all will be revealed to you and you will instinctively know what to do about it all.

This picture shows a spirit form enveloped in wisdom and spiritual gifts, working in many different ways whenever the need arises.

This is how you are. You can always help a fellow being, not necessarily by passing on information, but by always knowing someone who can do just that. You do not need to know about quantum physics, for example, but you know someone who does, and here is your purpose as you can always guide an enquirer in the right direction for that information to be found.

This is the way your life has gone at each stage in the development of your awareness and you have been happy in all you have done.

Now people will be coming into your life, people with other different skills and they will be guided to others through you – a continuation of what you have always done.'

'You must go ahead as we are planning to do. Along the way you will meet people who wish to push their ideas on to you. Be aware of this but do not antagonise them. They mean well. It is just that they are going along a different route.

We shall be with you along your pathway and guide you to a safe and joyous end. Do not be afraid.'

An example of this follows:–

AN AWKWARD SITUATION

At one point in my life I was asked to send something through the post to a third party on behalf of an acquaintance.

After much persuasion I agreed, but not before I had insisted that the sender should dictate to me the message he wished to send. I took it home, wrote a letter of explanation on his behalf, packaged it and posted it, all the time feeling very uneasy about the whole thing.

The person concerned was quite able to write a letter and I had actually given him the address. Also it was a subject I had no wish to become involved in.

Following this I received this message:–

'We want you to know that we are pleased with the way you handled this situation.

You were put into an awkward position but you handled it tactfully. You have done as you were asked and you must be aware that you are the type of person who can be easily taken for granted and be put upon. Do not allow this to happen.

Stand your ground. You have a very busy pathway to follow that is your own. Each person must be responsible for his own decisions along his own pathway and will not learn the lessons of life if he takes advantage of others.

You have been tested in this way many times in your life when you have been 'piggy-in-the-middle'. You have the strength to go forward in a positive way. others must learn to have that quality within themselves and not always to rely on others.

Be on your guard when you come across a situation like this again. No lessons are learnt if, in adversity, someone else is brought in to do the awkward and unpleasant tasks.

You have had a reminder that there are still people willing to take advantage of you if you allow it. You will be ready next time.

Sometimes it is better for a person to be rejected. He then has to learn to take the responsibility for his own actions – and he then learns how to manage his own life more efficiently.'

CONSIDERED THOUGHT

'It is not wise to jump to conclusions. If you give considered thought to an idea or suggestion then a positive answer can always be the outcome.

Never rush into anything without giving it a considered thought. You will be saved much anguish and possibly a lot of embarrassment.

Do not be too eager to solve other's problems. You need to think the situation out thoroughly before stepping in.

Do remember that you are each where you are to learn new lessons, and some of those can only be done to that person's advantage if the solution comes from within him/herself. Then a lesson has been well and truly learnt – and will be remembered next time a similar situation arises.'

TRAVELLING

'You are going to be very busy soon. You will be travelling around to places you have never visited before and will find it tiring but enjoyable – more new experiences. Rest when you can. You need to have plenty of energy for what is ahead, but rest assured we shall be with you.'

WORLDLY POSSESSIONS

'Apples where there are orchards' – so they say.

Many people who use their money or possessions wisely do enjoy life. They don't need to continually want for more, as do those who waste it then expect others to provide for them.

We all have as much as we need to make our lives comfortable. If used wisely we shall be at ease with everyone and never bitter.

Live life to the full within the restrictions of what is available to you. Don't envy others what they have. You are special in as much that you have a designated pathway.

Each one has his own pathway. Yours is right for you. Don't be misled. Go ahead. Each one's pathway is right for that person but not right for you at this time.

Be warned and don't be tempted to follow what in your heart you know is not right for you.'

Gradually it had become noticeable to me that contact with certain other people was becoming less frequent. Interests which we had both shared seemed no longer to be important. The degree of commitment there had been previously was deteriorating and one or the other of us had gone off in a new direction.

We discussed this and understood each others feelings, but Spirit spelt it out in a way which made the reason for it to be much more understanding and acceptable.

'You have to say 'goodbye' to past colleagues now. You are on a new road towards the future. Past acquaintances will be left behind you and will go forward on a different pathway from yours.

Do not feel concerned about this. They, like you, have started along a new pathway. All your pathways in life lead to new beginnings and those you meet as you travel along them are there so that you experience new understandings for future growth and awareness towards a fully spiritual goal.

When you have that knowledge, the task of those you have met has been fulfilled and it is then time to go in another direction and meet, and work with, a new set of people who can enlighten you in that direction.

The pathway you are on is smooth and long and you are finding it interesting and enjoyable. More of what you hear from others is now understandable to you. Things you never thought you would agree with, you do now. Go ahead –

LISTEN and HEAR and UNDERSTAND and FEEL FULFILLED'

MAKING ASSUMPTIONS

'It is not always wise to make assumptions as conditions can change and a whole reversal of feelings can cause the most unexpected things to occur.

If you had chosen not to have your reflexology done today you would have lost a chance to understand how things always work out in life. You have met Janet along this pathway and you are both on the same 'wave length'. You will travel together along this passage for a while and develop an understanding and an awareness which will benefit you both.'

'You now know what your life will be from now forwards – a very varied and interesting time. As our contact with you develops you notice how much more confident you become when relaying our messages.'

'We will help you during this coming year to understand more about the workings of Spirit and prove to you that you can rely on us. We will not let you down. Trust us.'

Contact with Spirit at this point was developed through a Development Circle (see page 83) where I learned to understand the mechanics of relaying messages to others.

LIFE ON OTHER PLANETS?

Imagine my surprise when sitting in the Church congregation I heard a voice from the pulpit saying most emphatically, "There is NO life on other planets. It has been scientifically proven. This NASA Space Probe is a complete waste of money."

A voice a couple of rows in front of me said, "I wonder what Elsie thinks of that?" Elsie was too polite to cause embarrassment at that point and speak aloud – but she did say "Rubbish!" under her breath.

I have wondered about this since I was young. If God made Eve to be a partner to Adam, and they had three sons, how did they manage to populate the earth when there were no girls for these lads to marry?

I never got any answers of course, because in my younger days sex education was unheard of, and children accepted what they were told. Little girls had to be 'seen and not heard', but if they asked questions of that kind any answer given that was followed by "Why?" was quickly terminated with, "Because I said so." So I soon learned to accept what I heard without question. But that particular one never went away.

Man must be a very conceited being if he thinks he is the only life form in the Universe. But it amazes me that so many are convinced that all life forms must be represented in a humanoid shape with 2 arms, 2 legs, a body and a head which should have 2 eyes, 2 ears, 1 mouth, 1 nose – and so on.

I suppose that being people we feel that we can understand the strange life forms we encounter during hypnosis, some regularly referred to as 'aliens', by trying to relate them to the perceptions we have of ourselves.

A good example of this is in Jenny Randles's book ABDUCTION (pub. Headline) p.193. When explaining what I have always described as 'Ghost-like Beings' Jenny's description was – 'Then 2 shapes appeared, silhouetted against the glow. Both were grey.

They were hazy but from her drawings could be taken as 'people'.

I have always believed that other planets are inhabited and although I have never been scientifically-minded I am sure that what I have always considered to be 'higher forms of intelligence' on those other planets would be adapted to whatever shape is the right one for them to live most easily with, on whatever happens to be there to sustain that life. Perhaps it is because of some inner latent

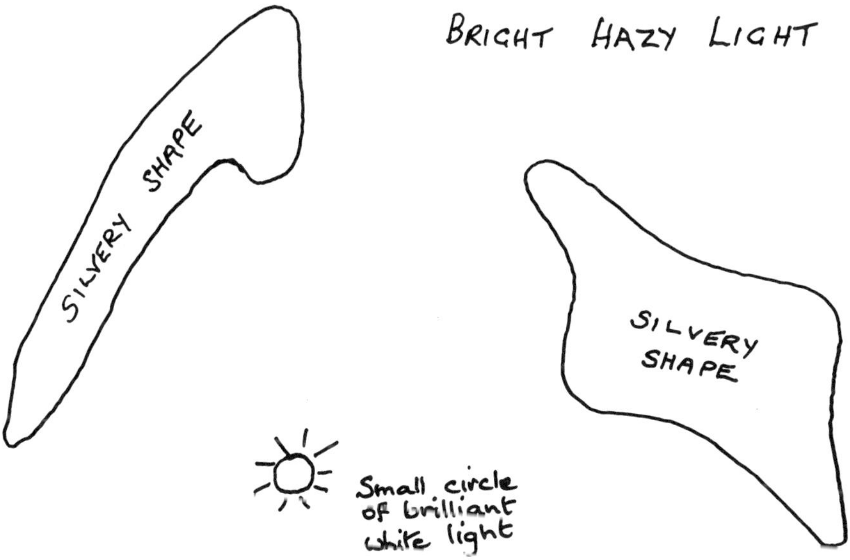

knowledge, that things which seem unbelievable to others, have a reasonable explanation to me.

In some cases that shape could resemble a gaseous blob and on meeting us they could programme us to perceive them as human beings, whilst at the same time they could perceive us as being one of their own kind.

I am sure this is not beyond the realms of probability.

During 1996/97 I joined a group on a course entitled DIRECT COMMUNICATION WITH THE SPIRIT WORLD and during this time we were given topics on which we were to find answers with help from our Spirit Companions.

These helped us to gain insight into that which is beyond the planet which we human Spirits now inhabit and after all those years here was my answer.

QUESTION
If the Physical World is not the final world – WHAT IS BEYOND?

ANSWER
'The Physical World in which you now live is one which combines both Human and Spirit components. It covers an experience which is necessary in the end for Spiritual growth.

After each incarnation to an earthly life the Spirit returns to another dimension commonly referred to as the Spirit World.

If more lessons are necessary for the growth then another 'visit' will be necessary until that ultimate growth is achieved.

The Universe is a vast space enfolding different times and different dimensions and the Spirit's 'return visits' also continue its growth.

In these areas of the Universe life continues but not in the way in which you are experiencing it when enclosed in a human body.

Learning continues and enhances the Spiritual Knowledge. We can then in many ways, through your mediumship and your willingness to allow us to channel through you, help those still on the earth plane.

In the Universe are many areas unknown to you where we rest and learn between our sojourns on earth. Here also our understanding is developing, and that which we learn there we can use to help a newly incarnated body on the earth planet.

Life in the Universe is different. We have different forms, and life on other planets than yours is created to be able to be sustained for that particular life style.

Our shapes will differ to be able to cope with different 'atmospheres' and different conditions which exist on other planets. Life is everywhere, not necessarily as you would expect it to be. The Spirit lives on.

In the Universe too are different dimensions where the Spirit rests at different stages on its journey towards the ultimate – the Supreme Being who is above us all. No one of us will achieve that level but we should all strive to achieve the highest we can.

Life is eternal for us all. We should all aim to achieve the highest level possible. Never give up. Every effort is worthwhile as you know.'

THE PURPOSE OF OUR EXISTENCE – AT THIS TIME

'While we were in the Spirit World waiting for another incarnation did we perhaps live in another form on another planet, in another time in space, on a different level of awareness – in a higher dimension?

Are we not here at this time for a certain purpose?

When we incarnate previous memories are erased. Not only previous earthly memories but also those of extra-terrestrial existence.

The awakening now of these previous extra-terrestrial memories of ours provides an answer to all that is to be.

All that has been, built up towards the preparation for a task which has to be performed to provide a new existence in, or a new time on this earth. We are here to do all of this this time around. This planet desperately needs assistance to raise its vibrations to a higher level. We have the ability to enable that to happen.

Spreading love and light to all will raise the peoples' awareness of spirit and help the transformation to go forward in a steady and positive manner with the least inconvenience to all.

Go forward, spread the truth and help all to understand. It is a worthwhile task – a valuable exercise in self-preservation. It costs nothing but love towards your fellow beings; and the reward will be greater than anyone at present can imagine.

Try it and reap the benefits. You will be pleasantly surprised.'

CONTACT WITH SPIRIT

INTRODUCTION

One date each year, apart from my birthday, is indelibly engraved on my memory. That is the 22nd November, the date on which, in 1978 I came into contact with a UFO and had what I now believe to be my first contact with the Spirit World.

As each year passed I always expected to have a replay of that experience, but it never happened, so it was a wonderful surprise when in 1994, 16 years afterwards, that my writings changed slightly and I realised that instead of writing 'I' my contact was writing 'WE'.

'In this picture you see the MOUNTAINS OF LIFE illustrating the strength you will need in the future, not only strength in health but strength in the conviction that what you say is the truth, for others to accept or reject. Whichever they choose will be their own choice.

Some of course, will hover on the brink of understanding as you know from past experience, but you must not falter. Go forth in strength and in knowing that all will be well with the world and with all those who genuinely have trust in Spirit.

Good Luck! This is the beginning. The future is planned and you will lead others forward. That is enough for now. Keep in contact. We will return.'

WE will return? Up to that point my only contact had been Ursula Brown (see p. 138) but she was certainly not with me at that point.

Remembering advice from the Development Circle (p. 83) I was attending I needed to ask questions.

"Who are you", I asked, curiosity getting the better of me. My pen immediately began to write.

'Your friendly ghost-like beings, as you have always called us,' came the answer. 'Our names are Jellicoe and Joseph. This is how you will know us.' (p. 138.)

Here I was in actual contact with the beings who had shown themselves to me on the day I had been hypnotised.

A reassuring message was to follow from Ursula.

'It is 16 years today since you saw your UFO, as you call it, and now you have had contact from Jellicoe and Joseph.

You will be learning now about them and their world so that you can tell people about other life in the Universe.

You will find all of this very interesting, but some people will find it very strange. The UFO witnesses will prove to you that you are all one, because they will be getting information through too.

Many people will not be happy that you will have the knowledge, especially those who have always felt that they have had the answers. Be aware of this because they will try to discredit you. But stand your ground and in time it will be proven that you have always spoken the truth.

You are selected to do this work. You will do it well. We will always be with you and you have some loyal support on your earth, the witnesses and many good friends who have this unique understanding.' Then I was offered a piece of advice –

'Do not fear ridicule.
It is the outward manifestation of ignorance.'

For a time Ursula continued to give me information as well and during the time we'd been together we had both grown in understanding where Spiritual communication was concerned.

This section contains information which I have been inspired to write since that anniversary of my UFO Close Encounter experience and are selected passages which outline my new Spiritual pathway since 22nd November 1994 – a pathway towards a most interesting and rewarding future for the benefit of mankind.

ENLIGHTENMENT

'The enlightenment of the world will be forthcoming in many ways. Our souls will rejoice and our hearts will overflow with love towards one another. Our minds will be as one. Our thoughts will all be positive.

We shall all sing praises to our God. We shall all be one. Love and peace will reign forever.'

LIFE IN SPACE

'The large expanse of sky you see is full of life. You have difficulty in understanding distance when you have no markers by which to measure.

The planets and stars, the sun and moon share the heavens, lighting up the days and nights. Everywhere there is life of some kind, not all as you would think of it, but everything lives and grows in its own form.

Some life forms grow in darkness, others need the light, some can live in water, others breathe in the air.

We all have different shapes and sizes to suit our particular needs and requirements. Variety in shape for each purpose in life is essential for each to exist and grow.'

OUR WORLD

'This gives you an idea of the living shapes of life on our planet.

We can move in many different ways. We can pass through time and space in the blink of an eye – as you say. We are very adaptable and journey far in a short space of time.

We are with you now. In time you will see us and hear us too. Be patient and all will be known to you. Love and understanding will be yours. You are not alone. The word is coming to your world and you will all be glad.'

'In your dreams we shall visit a wide open area which is full of exciting things to do and see. Plants grow there but they are not as yours on earth.

'This is the way they would be represented to humans who visited our planet – a world of different shapes, both spiky and smooth-edged.

They are many-coloured and always make us feel cheerful. You will find them to be breathtaking.

There on the earth they grow in the air. We have an atmosphere on our planet. You will learn to adapt to life with us. We are training you in your sleep.

Our houses are not like yours. We do and make everything with our minds. Whatever we think we have or need we find we do have or do get. If we need a cover we think it and have it. If we feel we want to eat, we think food and we are no longer hungry – so different from the complex methods you have on the earth.

Our spaceships travel long distances in the blink of an eye. Our landscapes are flat or mountainous whatever you think them to be, they will be. To return to earth will seem very strange after you have spent time with us. All of your modern ways will seem so old fashioned.

You will come soon. We shall welcome you.'

OUR HOME

'Our home is in outer space in a constellation called Ufdashadioux and we are in the ninth dimension. On our planet we do not look like human beings but when we visit your earth we represent ourselves to you in a like form so that you will know that we come in friendship and we will be welcomed by you.

The vehicles in which we travel are of many different shapes and sizes and can travel much faster than any vehicle on your earth. That is the reason they appear to disappear. Our acceleration rate is very speedy.

We come in love and friendship and will help all who are willing to help to preserve the earth to do so. It is important that we do this because should the earth, or any other planet in the universe deteriorate or disintegrate it will cause a loss of balance cosmically, and we shall all suffer. Please accept our help. It is for the benefit of everyone.'

US

'You often wonder what we are like to look at. You hear so many stories from other people, some of which can be very scary. But you need not worry. However we represent ourselves to you will be with an understanding that we come in peace. A physical representation is not important. What will be important is that you will not fear our presence. You have met us many times in your sleep state and know us as well as we know you. You will not be afraid for there is nothing for you to fear.

We are all working together for the same cause – to awaken all previous memories of those who have spent many times in many varying degrees of understanding in different times in space and in different levels of dimension. You all have an accumulation of wisdom and understanding of Spiritual ways, which you have gathered during these times. A wonderful combination of many types of knowledge which have been built up during these times when previous knowledge and understanding has been added to and broadened in order to fulfil that which is, the normal soul growth in every Spiritual Being.

No one of us will ever achieve the ultimate which the Great One has achieved, but we should strive to reach that which is possible in order to give dedicated service to our Lord. No effort in this is too small and no effort is too great. To do one's best is all that is expected. The satisfaction received from the effort given is always very worthwhile and greatly appreciated.

Every step along the way is one step nearer the ultimate goal. The end is very near. You have not far to go. It is worth the dedication and the effort towards complete fulfilment.

Continue along the way. You will have the strength. The reward will justify the effort.

OUT INTO SPACE

'Come with us on a journey through the cosmos, out into space at a speed faster than light. Out beyond the stars twinkling in your galaxy to a land you have yet to see.

Life exists everywhere in the universe though not exactly as you know it. Different types of life can only exist in certain types of atmosphere. That on your planet Earth is suitable for the existence of human beings. When we visit you we must adapt to your earthly conditions. When you come to visit us you will find that you will be able to adapt to ours. We shall help you of course.

We travel through space and see places light years away from your home, many lights in the sky (stars you would think of them as being). What you see from our spaceship's windows you marvel at. It is a scene which is new to you. You are in awe of it all.

This now, but one day it will be home again and you will feel you have never been away.

Until then you have work to do to prepare the people on your planet for devastation which will lead to the evacuation of the earth while it is upgraded to within a higher dimension.

Your work has started. Already you are telling the truth about us and people are listening to your words. You are preparing talks now for later on when people in different types of groups will expect a different kind of information.

All that you will need will be given to you. You will be prepared by us, and everyone who hears will know that is the information they have been waiting for.

A very busy and successful year lies ahead for you – a year of happiness, contentment and satisfaction. Good Luck.'

THE BLACK HOLE

'You have been giving much thought to 'The Black Hole' – terminology which is of man's definition to describe, in a way he understands, something which he has never experienced, because if he had travelled into it he would not have been able to return to tell you about it.

It is a vast expanse of space through which extra-terrestrial travel can take place, but nothing of human origin would be able to counteract. Your science has not yet reached that degree of competence.

Understanding of such areas comes to human beings through contact made with the Spirit World. We can explain but you do not necessarily understand. Your extra-terrestrial memories are returning but at a pace which we control. You must be able to have a complete understanding at each stage of your awakening before advancing to the next one.

Comprehension is difficult without a visual perception and that we shall bring to you in time. For now, at your present level of understanding, you are able to take that which we have allowed your mind to know.

You are doing well at this pace. Stay calm and more knowledge will come to you and as you progress it will be more easily assimilated.'

PHILOSOPHY

'Be brave, be strong, and adversity will fly to the winds. New and exciting things will be met along your pathway.

Not all you expect to happen will happen. Some things are not right for you at this time. Do not be disappointed. Everything happens for a reason and when the time is right you will know. We shall tell you and you will be ready.'

SPACE

'Tonight we shall go way out beyond the stars to the lands that you will come to know again in time.

Here you will meet old friends from the times past when you sojourned in these realms, lands full of life and overflowing with love and energy.

A place of peace where there are no upheavals of any kind, and life is full of wonder. Pleasures abound – all so different from the life you lead on planet Earth.

But a new awakening is around the corner for your people, one of understanding and concern for that which now is obvious. Change for the better must come for happiness to be everywhere. Sadly there are so many who do not want this yet.

The wise ones know the time is fast approaching for this change to happen. Much work has to be done to set this in motion. The journey is long and hard-going and the time is too short.

Set the ball in motion and let the news multiply.'

Over the years that followed that 'right time' arrived and many new talents were given to me.

The ways in which these have developed are described in the next section of this book under the heading of PASSAGES OF DISCOVERY.

PASSAGES OF DISCOVERY

AN INTRODUCTION TO PSYCHIC EVENTS

John was reading the *Daventry Express,* our local newspaper. Suddenly he looked up.

"There's a Psychic Event on in Daventry this weekend," he said quite casually.

"What's a Psychic Event?" I asked.

"I don't know," came a quick reply, "But you've become interested in some very strange things just lately. There's bound to be something there which will interest you."

So out of curiosity I went, and found myself stepping into a completely new world, one of mysticism and magic which turned out to be the beginning of another new chapter in my life. There were meditation tapes, crystals, the pendulum, psychic portraits and art, readings from tarot and playing cards, graphology, numbers – and a bookstall containing some about UFOs. I really had no idea where to start.

I stood alone in the entrance to a large room in what was then the John O'Gaunt Hotel and decided to work in a clock-wise direction talking to each person present, hoping they would be willing to explain to me what it was that they had come to do.

The first gentleman told me about meditation tapes. I had never meditated and could not understand why he emphasised that if I bought one I should not listen to it in the car.

A lady was spreading cards on the table in some kind of pattern and she said they were tarot cards. I couldn't see how they could possibly tell her things about me.

The two stalls selling crystals really fascinated me. I learned on one that a pretty blue stone was lapis lazuli, really lovely sounding words, so I bought one on a silver chain to wear as a pendant.

On the other I learned that one suspended on a piece of twisted wool was a pendulum. This was something I felt I could possibly use, that was of course if I could master the technique. So I bought one which came with a set of instructions.

The psychic artist would draw a portrait of a family member or a Guide, "using the colours in your aura," she said. I had never heard of an aura but I agreed and she drew a remarkable likeness of my maternal grandmother who had died when I was about seven years old. Later I found a photograph which proved it to be her and I was very impressed.

The bookstall was another surprise. Why did it include books about UFOs? Where was the connection?

Yes I had driven under something which others had categorised as a UFO, but what had that got to do with all these strange things I was encountering at a Psychic Event?

Over the years which followed I was to find that it had been the introduction to a very interesting change in my way of life.

THE DEVELOPMENT OF HEALING

MARY

In 1984 due to ill-health, it became necessary to retire from my post as Head of the Daventry Teachers' Centre. I had been diagnosed as having spinal spondylosis with osteoporosis in my neck, also cataracts growing in both eyes.

My Doctor told me that I would finish up in a wheelchair and have a dowager's hump. Even so he was concerned that I should not vegetate and suggested that I should join a craft class. I needed no encouragement to do this as it was a hobby I had always enjoyed and as such a class had just started in Weedon I promptly signed up.

It was there that I met a lady named Mary Earp and an immediate friendship developed. Not only did we share a love of craftwork but we both had arthritic problems and cataracts and I was later to find that she would be the Medium and Spiritual Healer who would guide me along that very same pathway, one which I did not understand, but which as time passed became easier to follow because of my UFO encounter.

Mary's interest in the UFO surprised me at the time. I could see no connection between the two. Then she invited me to go along one evening to the Development Circle (p. 83) she had formed at her home. I had been asked to explain to the group what had happened to me on 22nd November 1978 as they felt strongly that there was a connection between UFOs and the Spirit World.

There I explained it all as I had done to many others over the years. They listened and expressed much interest. I was asked many questions and I left that meeting not understanding why I also then felt that there definitely could be a connection between the two.

Later Mary asked me to join her Healing Circle and gradually it all became more comprehensible to me. And, as the years passed, becoming a Medium, a Healer, a Psychic Artist and a Dowser all developed as I became more understanding of the ways of Spirit.

I wasn't feeling very well
But still went off to sew.
One new student joined the class
And soon rapport did grow.

We both had pains in back and neck,
Arthritis was to blame.
I'd found an understanding friend
And Mary was her name.

A very special lady
She turned out to be,
Her interests went far deeper
Than the others – I could see.

She told me things about myself
I did not understand.
But she could see what I could not –
And gently held my hand,

Leading me slowly forward
Along a pathway new,
She guided me and taught me,
Comprehension slowly grew.

Encouragement was given
To tread the Spiritual way
And develop my gift of Healing
Understanding more each day.

Then she married Peter
And he's a Healer too.
Together they deepened my interest
And stronger my confidence grew.

It's thanks to their continuous help
I'm where I am today,
Able to help the sick to feel
Comforted in every way.

HEALING

On the day it was agreed with a friend that we should meet in Rugby to celebrate her birthday, she also arranged something else for us to do.

"You'll need a 90 cassette," she said – and would add nothing more, except to say that it was to be a surprise. And indeed, a bigger surprise I could not possibly have imagined. We were to visit a Medium and have a reading.

It was a few months before this at a Craft Class that I had befriended Mary who had said she was a Medium and Healer. I had no idea what she meant and I always found that my ignorance on any subject was much less obvious if I didn't ask questions. Now, of course, I know that she would not have been offended if I had done so, nor would that visit (with my cassette) have resulted in such disbelief.

It was to be my first visit to such a person and although I had always felt that my mother, when she was alive, understood much that I now class as Spiritual, I was not aware of the terminology on that day. But, to me, all new experiences can become an introduction towards further learning, so I met Charles Chapman with great expectations of the possibility that a new interest might develop as I travelled further into my retirement years.

I listened attentively as he explained what was happening, as he brought in my relatives, and how my father became the spokesman for the group. It was fascinating. So much information about my past and that concerning my future was flowing freely. There was no way in which I could take it all in as I listened and I remember thinking it was a very good thing that it was all being recorded.

An hour and a half later I emerged from the room completely stunned. I had heard things about my life that had happened, and were still happening in order to form a basis for what was to be in the future.

My mind seemed to be in a whirl. Such a lot to be put into some kind of perspective. So much I didn't understand. How I needed my mother's help to put it into a way in which I would then feel I could be in total control.

I drove home with all these thoughts racing through my mind. This was something I really had to sleep on. Perhaps the following morning it would all slot into place, but the only words which I remembered kept ringing through my ears.

"You will come to Mediumship through Healing. You have the gift and it would be a pity not to develop it."

I knew I had to find out what had been meant by HEALING and I knew also that I then had to start asking questions.

Several days after this I felt I was ready to accept what I had been told so I listened to the tape and was truly amazed. But, as with all things, an answer to one question always seems to leave me with another question, which then also needs an answer. However as I listened the following words from the tape also became prominent.

"If you need more help in understanding what I have told you, come and see me again. I shall be only too happy to help you."

That offer could not be ignored. I really did need help to understand what was happening to me. The palms of my hands had started to become very hot at times and the tips of my fingers tingled too – strange sensations for a person whose hands were normally so cold whatever the weather was like. I knew in my heart that I must do something about it. Another visit to Charles Chapman was obviously essential.

Having been a teacher for so long the appropriate next step was preparation, so I made a list of every question which came into my mind and to which I felt an answer was required so that I could more fully understand what was expected of me. Also I mentioned the suggestion that I was to become a Healer to anyone interested enough to listen, just as I had done regarding the UFO sighting immediately after that had happened 12 years before.

But whereas that had been met with disbelief and ridicule this time my news was met with interest. To my surprise I found that most were already Healers themselves. Each offered advice, some which I could understand and some which I could not.

This was then added to my questions list for further clarification.

Needless to say Charles expected my phone call. Again I arrived with a 90 cassette and I spent an even more interesting time discussing my questions and familiarising myself with detailed answers to them all. It was a 2-way process which enabled me to fully understand this new pathway along which it was obviously intended that I should be travelling.

It was at the time of these visits that a very dear friend of ours became very ill with cancer and after my visits to him I had found that I was feeling uncomfortable myself.

It was through this that I came to understand that by visiting him I was able to pass Healing to him without being conscious of doing so. Because of the love I had for his family the Healing energies were flowing freely through me and I was able to help to relieve some of his pain without, at that time, realising I could be doing so.

This was my introduction to the practical side of Healing and was followed by many examples in which my friends and members of my family benefited.

Over the years which have followed encouragement came in many forms and culminated in an offer of Sponsorship from Mary Earp and Peter Maceachrane to become a Healer with the National Federation of Spiritual Healers, then with help through this from a Healing Group in Northampton, becoming a member of Mary's Healing Circle, also encouragement from other Healers later, I am able to summarise the advice I have collected over the years regarding the questions which were raised in my mind following that first visit to Charles Chapman.

One night in bed my hands were hot,
Why I did not know.
A different kind of heat it was
From that which made me glow
And feel warm all over.
This was centred in my hands,
And then my fingers tingled too –
Wonderment expands!

A visit to Charles Chapman
Gave me a big surprise.
"The gift of healing you have," he said.
"To develop it would be wise.
To be able to help others
Is a truly wonderful thing.
The pleasure you receive from it
Encompasses everything."

My husband too agreed with this,
And with his full support
The decision to go ahead was made
Enthusiasm caught!
"Spirit works in wonderful ways," was said,
And so it turned out to be,
For all around I soon found
Were Healers advising me.

I'd joined a group of people
So wonderful to know.
A positive attitude to life
Within them all did glow.
Encouragement they gave me
To develop in every way,
Each pathway led to something new
And I learned more each day.

This 'work' is really a pleasure
And Spirit is my Guide,
Knowing exactly what has to be done
And always by my side.
For they are happy to use me
As a channel through which to heal
And we do help each other –
It's a complementary deal.

QUESTIONS AND ANSWERS

"You will come to Mediumship through Healing," I had been told.

This came at a time when I was learning to accept my own Doctor's forecast for the future – "I can give you 8 painkillers a day for the rest of your life, but you must be prepared to finish up in a wheelchair, with a dowager's hump."

If this was correct how could I possibly start a new career into that of a Healer. It was a new and exciting prospect and would be a real challenge in any condition, but I needed to know more about what would be involved.

I talked about it to anyone who would listen and these people seemed to fall into two groups. There were those who were Healers themselves and who offered much advice, and there were those who asked what it would all involve. To this I had no answer, but I knew in my heart that it was something that I had to look into and examine in great detail before making a final decision to go ahead – and that is what I did.

During my second visit to Charles Chapman one question led to another and I have summarised in a simple way the information and advice I have received during my years as a Healer since 1990.

QUESTIONS

- You tell me that I am a Healer. What exactly does Healing mean?
- How is a link formed?
- How is Healing done?
- Is there a special way to give Healing?
- How long does Healing take? If I continue Healing until my hands cool down, is that all right?
- How long should a Healing session last?
- Do the effects of Healing stop as soon as the Healing session stops?
- Can I give a patient too much Healing?
- Can I give Healing too often to the same patient?
- Is the best Healing done in the first five minutes of the session?
- How can I tell whether the Healing is working or not?
- If there are two Healers helping one patient, does one negate what the other does?

- When two or more people are giving Healing to the same person each would have his own group of Spirit Helpers.

  If this was not my patient would the other Healer's Spirit Doctors feel that mine were interfering?
- How will I know the Healing energies are transferred? Will I be shown?
- Will my Spirit Helpers show themselves to me?
- I would love to be able to help friends and relatives who are ill but live too far away to visit regularly. Will I be able to help them?

ABSENT/DISTANT HEALING

- TRANCE Healing
- Do I need to attend courses in order to develop as a Healer?
- HEALING or MARRIAGE?

ANSWERS AND ADVICE

QUESTION: You tell me that I am a Healer. What exactly does HEALING mean?
ANSWER: The basic principle is for you to establish a link between the patient and the Spirit World. Healing is a process of love and Spiritual awareness.

QUESTION: How is a link formed?
ANSWER: Healing is a process of learning to work together, having full faith and trust in your Spirit partners. We vibrate at our speed but the Spirit world vibrates at a much faster speed. So you as a Healer are a kind of transformer, receiving in your mind Spirit's slowed-down vibrations, and then transferring them to the normal wavelength of the earth plane.

Everything is energy – vibrations. If you have a cheerful voice Spirit will use that vibration. This is mediumship, know that you cannot go wrong if you help people. There is nothing to fear when doing Spiritual work. You cannot do any harm.

QUESTION: How is Healing done?
ADVICE: You should heal in your own way. if you feel you just want to hold the patient's hand then that is the right way for that patient.

It is not necessary to touch an organ or even to be near it. The Healing will flow to whichever area it is required. The Healing link is through you.

Just sitting and talking forms a link and you are giving Healing. Therapies and counselling do too. A bond of Spiritual love has been established. You have contact. That is all that is necessary for Healing to take place.

Also you do not need to be in direct contact with a person for that person to feel the benefit. Healing can be given from a distance. This is known as Absent (or Distant) Healing and is just as effective as any other method.

QUESTION: Is there a special way to give Healing?
ANSWER: You can't tell a person how to heal. Some heal by colour, others by vibrations, with crystals and all manner of things. Let Spirit lead you.

The only thing you must insist on is that no woman's chest or any private parts are touched by a Healer of the opposite sex. You will reflect Healing in those areas.

QUESTION: How long does Healing take? If I continue Healing until my hands cool down, is that all right?
ANSWER: Yes. Sometimes relief from pain will seem to happen almost immediately. Sometimes it will take much longer and will require several sessions of treatment.

QUESTION: How long should a Healing session last?
ANSWER: In any Spiritual work you cannot define 'time' because time as we know it doesn't exist in the Spirit World. Time there is a progress, or curing, or Healing, or informing to a person in a Reading.

The requirement of one patient may be half-an-hour, another may be two hours. You cannot know.

A person sits in a Healing chair. How long he is required to be there is between the Spirit World and the patient. The Healer is the 'plug in the wall'.

We are the instruments being used by the Spirit World. We don't know what is wrong with a patient, so we can't say how long the healing will take. The Spirit world controls that.

QUESTION: Do the effects of Healing stop as soon as the Healing Session ends?
ANSWER: No, it goes on for as long as it is necessary to complete that part of the treatment.

My own example of TRANCE HEALING (p. 72) proves this point.

QUESTION:Can I give a patient too much Healing?
ANSWER:No. You are the link between the Spirit World (the giver) and the patient (the receiver).

Only Spirit knows exactly what is needed in each case and treats each individual patient accordingly. You are there to make that specialist treatment available.

QUESTION: Can I give Healing too often to the same patient?
ANSWER: No. Healing is not an earthly thing. The amount required is controlled completely by the Spirit World

QUESTION: Is the best Healing done in the first 5 minutes of the session?

ANSWER: No. All treatment given by Spirit during a healing session, no matter what time elapses, is equally essential to that patient.

QUESTION: How can I tell whether the Healing is working or not?
ANSWER: Try not to judge the results of being used for healing. You don't know. Don't get despondent if you think the patient looks worse this week than he did the last time you saw him. You do not know what is going on in that person's life. He could have been in a far worse condition. Maybe he has let himself go.

Sometimes a sick person resents being ill, thinking it to be undeserved. This is a mental attitude which can definitely be a barrier to any Healing sought or to the progress in getting well.

Facing up to the reality of the situation, seeking for and admitting the cause is more likely to prove beneficial.

God helps those who help themselves. We must contribute. It is like earthly medicine. After an operation if you don't want to get over it, then you won't. It's entirely up to you in the end.

QUESTION: If there are two Healers helping one patient, does one negate what the other does?
ANSWER: No. Each will be Healing in love and will complement the other in order that the patient will feel the benefit from the Healing session.

You cannot over heal and you cannot create a negative to one another.

QUESTION: When two or more people are giving Healing to the same person each would have his own group of Spirit helpers.

If this was not my patient would the other Healer's Spirit Doctors feel that mine were interfering?
ANSWER: No, that is a human attitude. Spirit is not of that nature. There are many Spirit helpers at each Healing session even if there is just one Healer present.

If several Healers help with the same patient it is all done in Spiritual love for the person who needs the Healing.

QUESTION: How will I know how the Healing energies are transferred? Will I be shown?
ANSWER: Maybe, but that will depend whether Spirit decides to show you or not. This is something which no one can guarantee. However, during one Healing session the following amazing thing happened.

As I stood behind the patient's chair with my hands on her shoulders it was as if I was actually sitting away from myself to my right side and I could see myself in profile as a black outline. Suddenly there was a strange feeling in my own head and I could see a golden ball of Healing energy within the outline of my head.

This went into my right shoulder and down my arm to the palm of my hand, then into the patient.

"That was a clairvoyant vision", I was later told by a Healer friend. "Spirit was showing you how they see you when they are working through you."

QUESTION: Will my Spirit Helpers show themselves to me?
ANSWER: This is something which no one can guarantee but you could be lucky – and I do believe that on one occasion I was.

This happened in 1990 during the time that I was coming to terms with the knowledge that I was becoming a Healer.

Another Healer and I were meeting regularly one night a week. We meditated, I practised my Healing on her, then we discussed any related subject which cropped up. On this particular evening we tried out our ability to do automatic writing and all I got were scribbles while she received a legible message.

It was then almost 12 years since my UFO Close Encounter and at 10.15 p.m. I was travelling along that same section of road. During the 5 minutes it took to reach home I was aware of a brightness in the sky which, within it, contained lights which changed shape 5 times as I watched. (See Appendix 3 for details.)

Following this my automatic writing became legible. The first words were ELSIE WELCOME and I learned that I had a Spirit Guide name MUKELIB, that he was a North American Indian and that he would be with me on the evenings we did our meditations, writing and Healing.

About one month after this I awoke to see a large ball of orangery-yellow light in the sky. This had a diagonal straight edge cutting off the top left-hand corner.

I watched as it moved downwards in the sky, lighting up the underside of the layers of cloud above it. Then I returned to bed, When nearly asleep I turned over and there in front of me a face appeared. It was a dark-skinned, heavily-lined, grey-haired face, that of a North American Indian.

My immediate reaction was to ask, "Mukelib, is that you?" There was no reply either spoken, or in my mind and the face faded away.

I have always felt it was right to believe that I did see Mukelib, my Spirit Helper who guided me into my new life as a Healer.

QUESTION: I would love to be able to help friends and relatives who are ill but live too far away to visit regularly.

Will I be able to help them?
ADVICE. Yes. Absent/Distant Healing is just as powerful as Contact Healing.

The condition of the world today is perhaps the lowest it has been in the history of the world with the brutality, the lust for sex, the violence; and Spirit does not have enough helpers on the earth plane.

You will find that if there is a grave necessity at a particular time, because your heart is so big to help people, they will open your channel. Hence you'll get a tremendous burning.

It may be for anybody anywhere in the world. Maybe they are healing somebody while they sleep, and because they cannot heal direct they are using you.

The following poem I received describes an experience I actually had and is appropriate at this point. (See also p. 77.)

It's 5 am and I'm awake
I wonder what to do.
Shall I get up and make a drink
Or stay in bed with you?

The desire to sleep has completely gone.
It's a feeling that is not new.
My hands and body are terrible hot.
It's Healing coming through.

Somewhere my Spirit Helpers know
There are people in dire need
Of their Specialist help, at this moment in time,
So use my channel as we've agreed.

A cup of tea won't help me
Now that I've cooled down again.
The Healing session is over
And has not been in vain.

For many folk that I don't know
And may well never see,
Have felt the benefit tonight
Of Spirit's work – through me.

A telephone conversation is Absent Healing too. Here Spirit will link you to a person and Healing will result. But you haven't opened your channel, have you? It is a natural thing for this to happen when the need arises – such as in this case:–

The lady I was speaking to on the telephone said she didn't feel at all well. She sounded so low and lacking in hope. The last time we'd met she was a very jubilant and buoyant person, full of confidence.

Now she was having difficulty in putting her thoughts into words. She was full of despair and she couldn't understand why.

I tried to keep my voice full of hope for a return to the person I'd met before and to make it obvious that I cared. She needed to talk. I had time to listen and to try to understand. I felt that I needed in some way to lift her hopes for her future, to assure her that she could again become that positive-thinking person.

When I first retired from work through ill-health I had experienced a period of deep depression. I found I cried seemingly for no reason at all. I could relate in some small way to her.

At that point suggestions seemed to come into my mind – positive thoughts – and I suggested them to her. I understood how difficult it is to be positive and cheerful when you are at your lowest ebb. It is much easier not to try.

Among other things we talked about writing small cheerful notes and putting them around the house. I had heard this suggested a few days before on the television, then as you pass them you read them and try to do exactly what they say.

She talked about her treatment and she suddenly said, "There are people there who are worse than I am."

"There you are," I said, "that's a positive thought of your own. You have noticed that your own health is better than some of the other patients. Your aim now can be to keep it at that level and to improve it."

The Healing process had begun. She was helping her body to heal itself. We talked for about 3/4 hour and a bee flew near to her. "I must let it out of the window," she said and she continued to describe what she was doing as she helped it fly away.

By then her speech was more coherent and she was obviously moving around. "I must get on now. I mustn't stay on the phone. I have a lot to do," she explained brightly and she terminated the call herself.

I am very conscious that in all cases such as this the Healing Spirits are with us as we talk. At the beginning of this conversation there had been gaps of silence, then subjects to discuss just came into my mind, very definitely and one at a time, for gentle discussion. Healing was given and received during that time, and proved yet again that even when it is at a distance it is very effective. I saw her a few weeks later and she was again her old self.

Her doctor had also changed her medication and as healing complements modern medical science in this case the combination had a beneficial reaction.

When the phone rings, in answer to the greeting, "Hello! How are you?" the reply is usually, "Fine, thank you." Possibly a predictable answer to such a question, but the tone of your voice can denote what might be the hidden but genuine response.

And when the reply includes another question such as, "Fine, but how are you?" it usually tells me that some kind of help is hoped for. but there's a hesitation regarding an actual request for it.

On one occasion, having got through the formalities I found a pain developing in my chest – a tightness which had not been there before I picked up the phone.

As we spoke it intensified and eventually I said, "Oh, excuse me a moment, I feel I need to burp" – and I did – an enormous one.

"Oh, that's much better," I said with genuine relief.

"Yes, it is," came a confident reply. "I've been needing to do that for some time, and it just wouldn't come. Thanks very much. I feel much better now." And to the relief of us both our conversation was able to continue along normal lines.

Sometimes I seemed to 'know' that help is needed and find that the person I have rung is feeling low at that time and in need of a cheerful input into their life.

It is very rewarding to hear the change in a person as the conversation develops. Perhaps it is something very simple that has caused that low ebb especially if they live alone. An outsider with a cheerful voice can raise the vibrations and bring that person back on to an even keel, again able to view the situation in a balanced way.

Absent Healing can occur in many ways and in this case it was I who was –
ON THE RECEIVING END

The phone rang. "Hello," said the caller, "how are you?"

Usually my reply would have been, "Fine thank you. How are you?" But on this occasion I'd been suffering from 'flu for the second time that year and this time it seemed to be accompanied by dizziness. A locum had diagnosed very high blood pressure and given me tablets which seemed to be making my condition worse.

Luckily my own Doctor had returned from his holiday and I had seen him that morning. He was very concerned about the diagnosis and had changed the medication. He suggested that I should return in 4 days time to see how things were going.

When this call came I was feeling at my lowest ebb, so my answer on that occasion was, "Not very well at all, actually," and I proceeded to describe what had happened.

I was immediately offered help and assured that I would be sent Healing energies after we had finished speaking.

This was done and almost immediately my energy level was raised and the dizziness lessened.

Four days later when I walked into my Doctor's surgery his first words to me were, "You look 200% better today than when I saw you last," and I answered truthfully, "And I feel it too."

Healers will always advise patients to seek help from their own doctor as it is known that Healing complements modern medicine.

This had been another very good example.

TRANCE HEALING

The only way I can describe this kind of healing is through personal experience. It is not something I practice myself.

After my visit to Charles Chapman one of the people I met who claimed to be a Healer herself told me many things about Healing and what it involved – and the most amazing thing I recall was that she had herself visited a Trance Healer many years before, following a mastectomy operation after which the medical profession had given her 6 months to live.

We had a mutual friend at the time whom she felt would also benefit from this kind of Healing and invited me to accompany them both in order to see this Healer at work. Out of curiosity I readily agreed, and it was decided that I should drive to the meeting and that one of the others would drive back.

As I had no idea what to expect I felt I should be the last to be treated and as we were all in the same room all the time I was able to familiarise myself with the procedure.

The patient sat on a stool and the Healer stood behind him. He said a short prayer, breathed very deeply several times, then spoke. His voice had changed completely. He had been taken over by his Spirit Helper who was then in complete control of the situation. A lady stood by the Healer's side with arms outstretched. I was later told that she was there to give extra power for the Healing process and protection to the Healer while he was in trance. I was fascinated.

When it was my turn and I was in a comfortable sitting position this 'different' voice asked, "And how can I help you, my dear?" Making a quick decision I decided to tell him about the problems I'd had with my back; problems which by then I had come to terms with, could cope with, and no longer thought of as problems.

"I had to retire from work about six years ago with spinal spondylosis," I began.

"No such thing," he announced very positively and proceeded to examine my spine.

"And I still have to wear a collar sometimes," I added.

Then I heard what sounded like the slapping of one hand against another, except that it sounded more like a crack and this happened four times altogether. Then he told me that I had been involved in a car accident when a young child and my need to wear a collar was not caused by 'wear and tear' (as my doctor had said) but because of a whiplash injury sustained in that accident.

He asked if I could recall anything like that happening, and I could. I must have been about seven years old when Dad jammed on the brakes of the car and I, sitting in the front passenger seat, had shot forwards towards the windscreen – and screamed. I remembered no pain at all, just being told off for screaming.

"Yes that's right," he said.

My fully relaxed body was then moved in a way in which I would never have thought possible. The top part of me was lifted and twisted around so that I faced 90° to the right, then 90° to the left of the normal sitting position, then it was relaxed. Immediately my head seemed to be lifted off my shoulders and turned in the same way. I cannot remember ever having been able to do that before, and during this whole session I felt no pain or discomfort at all.

My instructions following this Healing session were to move carefully and to soak for a quarter of an hour in a hot bath containing a handful of seasalt, twice a day for a week, and after each bath to rub Witch Hazel on to my back. This I did do.

On the day after the Healing I woke to find my spine stiff from top to bottom. It was as if I was wearing a corset and had heavy weights on my shoulders. I seemed to have a new upright shape. Then about two days later the stiffness started to wear off a little at a time from my neck downwards, until a week later when the last piece at the base loosened up.

I learned later that my 'spinal spondylosis' was really four displaced vertebrae and that what I thought sounded like 'cracks' was actually the tearing of muscles as each vertebrae was realigned. Someone said that I should have stayed in bed for the whole of that first week, but I didn't. I did move carefully though. I had to, the stiffness in my back made certain of that. Everyone with whom I came into contact said that during that time I looked awful. I have admitted it since, though I wouldn't at the time, I felt far from well after that visit, but I carried out the instructions to the letter and my back is now very straight and I have not needed to wear my collar since.

I realise now, though I didn't at the time that what happened in that half-an-hour or so on that day must have been equivalent to major surgery, but I felt no pain at all so did not realise the significance of it.

On other occasions since, I have had trance healing on my arthriticky toes which was very painful for about one minute, and then it was over. I used to go dancing in the evenings following that treatment.

Also I have had my eyes 'polished' and since that treatment my cataracts have stopped growing for a time, then developed very quickly and the first is now ready for removal.

QUESTION: Do I need to attend courses in order to develop as a Healer?
ADVICE: No, you don't need a development class. A better word for development is awareness. It means becoming aware of what you are capable, or will be capable of doing, or carrying out with your Spirit Friends.

Nobody can define how, what or where because we are individuals and so are our Spirit friends. Nobody can say you will do it this way or that way. Healing is a private and beautiful thing between you and your Spirit helpers.

You must remember too that you are equally important, because without you your Spirit helpers cannot work, so never feel embarrassed to take half the credit.

Spirit is very pleased with the whole concept of your life. They want you to remember not to bring back the sadness of the tremendous hurdles you've had to overcome, particularly when you feel a bit down. Be positive. Just remember the success you've had. It hasn't been easy to stick at it and overcome those tremendous hurdles that seemed insurmountable at the time.

That's going to help you an awful lot. It will also help you to push people away who are trying to push you too quickly or want you to take on too much.

Remember HER – The lady you see in the mirror.

Remember that you are very important. The more you work for people, for God, for Spirit, the more important you are, because if you drop out a lot of people suffer. They suffer without your help.

As you well know the Spirit World doesn't have anywhere near the number of helpers or workers they need. It's tragic because those they have are overworked.

Remember all of this, then you will remain well-balanced. Do be careful. Don't go over the edge or you'll pay the penalty. You must have your "off" times, getting away and enjoying yourself, not just a holiday, but relax in whatever ways you enjoy. Go out with your husband to dance, to a show or whatever.

That way you'll keep the whole balance of your mind and your body happy and strong because there's an awful lot for you to do. I don't know if you are aware of that fully but you have got on to a very hard, fast belt now. You have developed a lot in the last 12 months. It isn't always easy, is it?

Later it became obvious that it would be wise to join a Healing Group and I found it very interesting to see how other Healers worked. It was also reassuring to learn that my technique met with no disapproval.

Mary and her husband Peter Maceachrane offered their sponsorship and with their guidance and continued encouragement from Charles Chapman I became a Healer Member of the National Federation of Spiritual Healers.

HEALING OR MARRIAGE?

During the time that my UFO Close Encounter was being investigated I met many researchers, and on one occasion I was very casually asked, "I don't know whether you realise it but your marriage could break up now."

I had assumed on that day that these particular people would be bringing positive news and would be able to explain what it was that I had driven under, and why it had been there above the road – but the forecast of a marriage breakup was completely unexpected.

"Why?" I had asked, in a state of disbelief. "Because your husband wasn't with you," I was told, "and many couples split up after something like this happens, because the one who wasn't there doesn't know how to cope with the reactions of the one who was involved."

Until recently I have never disclosed that information to anyone, not even to my family but it did have an effect on the way I behaved afterwards, I told myself that I must be seen to behave normally and became very conscious of over-emphasising my responses to other people's greetings. I smiled broadly at everyone I met, exuding a very friendly nature, and never brought the subject into any conversation at all – in fact if UFOs were mentioned I would walk away. I just couldn't bear the thought that one day someone would say to me, 'I told you so.'

This went on for 12 years and then I became a Healer and many of the reservations mentioned in this section began to surface, one of them being my relationship with my husband.

A divorced lady Healer who took me under her wing decided that together we would start a Healing Centre in a neighbouring village, the idea being that she would supply the premises and I would do the Healing.

It soon became apparent that this was to become a full-time occupation, but I had family commitments and a social life. John and I had both retired from work, my health had improved considerably and in retirement, with our sons married and living away we were enjoying a togetherness which had been impossible before, when over so many years we had both worked such long irregular hours.

So you can imagine what a shock it was to hear my prospective Healing partner, when laying down the ground rules to our proposed venture saying, "of course you must be prepared for your marriage to break up now."

The first time John and I had worked through the UFO experience and although some-one who has not had that experience cannot be expected to fully understand it in one who has, we each respected the other's feelings regarding it and it became part of our lives.

Now here it was again. John knew about the Healing. He didn't understand it any more than he understood UFOs, but he took each new experience in his stride and fully supported me each time something new came along.

So when I next visited Charles Chapman my final question was – WHAT ABOUT MY MARRIAGE? WHERE WILL THAT FIT INTO MY FUTURE AS A HEALER?

Without the slightest hesitation his immediate response was very definite –

"YOUR MARRIAGE COMES FIRST."

And as life continues so does my Mediumship and my work as a Healer, both sustaining and strengthening our marriage and giving John and me a deeper understanding of all that has happened in the past.

THE PASSING

Some people wonder why, when their loved ones are in receipt of Spiritual Healing, life as we know it will cease to exist.

This is because Healing cannot prolong life, but it does help towards a peaceful passing when the time comes.

* * * *

The following example would be equally applicable under the heading of Absent Healing. (See also p. 69.)

Whilst attending a Dancing Class I suddenly became so hot it was almost unbelievable. There was no warning at all.

A fellow dancer who is also a Healer was administering Healing to a member of the group at that time and I thought that this heat within me could be to help her – but it was so intense, obviously for someone in much more need than that particular lady.

I wondered if it could be for someone I knew or perhaps someone I had never met. I remarked on it to my partner.

After about five minutes my body temperature was back to normal and we danced away. The lesson finished and we went home, thinking no more of it.

About half-an-hour later the phone rang. The caller was telling me that her brother had died suddenly about an hour before. I looked at my watch. That had been the time I had remarked on the excessive heat that I had felt.

The Healing had been for that gentleman to ease his passing into the Spirit World.

* * * *

THE WASPS

It was a warm sunny morning in August and I was giving healing to an elderly gentleman who was in the final stages of lung cancer. The windows were open and scent from the colourful flowers in the garden wafted into the room.

He sat comfortably in his armchair by the empty fireplace and dozed as the healing energies were administered. All was calm and peaceful.

Listening to the birds' songs coming from the garden I realised that I could also hear among them, a buzzing sound within the room. A wasp had flown in through the open window. I am not a lover of wasps. To me their behaviour seems to be unpredictable, but as my patient seemed unconcerned I decided that if it avoided us then I would ignore it.

It flew around us and across the room. Then another joined it – and another. I looked towards the window and could see several more flying in. They came into the room and around us, swooping up and down as they passed, and gradually they were joined by what seemed like an endless number, all following the same routine.

I continued with the healing as I was strangely aware that they meant us no harm.

After a while I realised that their number was increasing noticeably and that not one was leaving. I began to be concerned in case we should be stung so the lady of the house brought in a jam-jar with a small amount of jam and half-filled with water which she placed on the window-sill by the open window.

Almost immediately one wasp flew over the jar and out through the window back into the garden. As if it were a signal, those remaining flew around us once more in a remarkably orderly fashion, then over the jam-jar and out to the garden until we were again alone in the room.

A few hours later that gentleman passed over and I have been left with a question:

'Had those wasps known that this was to happen and had they come to pay their last respects to him?'

If so, I feel very privileged to have witnessed it all.

LIFE AFTER 'DEATH'

'Here we shall talk about life after death as you refer to it in human life.

Your spirit is attached to your earthly body by a silver chord which, when life ceases as you know it today, detaches itself from that body and passes on to progress into the next world.

That next world is the world of Spirit, where life continues and Spirit develops until it is ready to embark on anothcr worldly incarnation.

During this time residence may be in a different form on a different planet, in a different time or in a different dimension, where new experiences occur to enhance the learning and knowledge which is stored for the growth of that spirit which is developing all the time towards a complete awareness of all that is part of this vast universe.

Each earthly body has all past knowledge from the Universe stored within it, but those memories are erased when incarnation on earth happens. But the time is near for those memories to be awakened so that all will be clearly understood about life outside planet earth.

We shall be unmasking these mysteries soon. You will be ready when the time comes and you will be pleasantly surprised how much information you have collected during this time.

You have travelled far in time and space and learned a great deal. We have been taking you in your sleep state where you have rejoined other souls on similar journeys.

The details will be made known to you when the time is right. It will be soon.'

LIFE GOES ON

THE WEDDING RING

This is an account of part of a reading given to me by a dear friend who is a Medium.

During the reading she said, "Your mother has come through and she is talking about two rings. Has she got two wedding rings?"

"No, but I have," I answered.

"Oh, yes it's you. Your mother is asking why you don't wear one of them any more."

I explained that it was because, as my hands got arthriticky the second one, which was much wider than the first would not pass over my swollen knuckles – but it also slipped off my little finger.

"Well, it's a pretty ring, your mother says you should show it off. Why not use it as a scarf ring?"

Then she pointed to my jacket which was on another chair. "Why am I pointing to your coat?" she asked.

"Because the ring you are talking about is in one of the pockets," I said.

I took my pendulum from my pocket. It was attached to a very long chain, so I had wound the other end of that chain around the ring making it easier to handle, and I explained this to her.

My mother then said that if she had had that ring SHE would "show it off" and that I should do the same.

Since that day I have worn it and now use a smaller ring also to ensure that it doesn't slip off my little finger.

What is remarkable about this account is that I was given this ring by my husband on our 21st Wedding Anniversary (1972) and my mother had died in 1962, ten years before it had been given to me. She had come through with messages for me before that date and I wondered why she should mention the ring at this particular time.

Then I realised. I was given this ring on my 21st Wedding Anniversary. This particular year (1993) I would be celebrating my 42nd Wedding Anniversary – another 21 years. How appropriate to mention it then and what a perfect example to prove that LIFE really does continue after death as we think of it.

The following example proves that our animals are equally important in the afterlife.

ANIMALS IN SPIRIT

About 2 to 3 months after John's cousin Irene died I awoke in the night to see her standing at the bottom of our bed.

"Elsie," she said, "I've just come to tell you that I've met Mother and Dad – and Anne is here." She sounded so happy.

And then she was gone.

Anne was Irene's daughter who had died when she was 5 days old. She would have been in her forties had she lived, and the dogs referred to were Scottish Terriers. As long as I had known them there was always one there. Each had lived until it died of natural causes, then it was replaced by another – and each one was called Jock.

TAKE TIME TO THINK

Take time to think – and
Fly to the ends of the earth.
There to sit and contemplate
The nature of our birth.
Of how we came to be here;
Of who has made us all;
Of everything so wonderful,
No matter how large or small.

So great are we that all things
Are controlled along our path.
A source of comfort and delight
Is what we are made of.
Happiness flows within us
Causing us to be glad.
It makes those we meet more happy
Leaving fewer to be sad.

And when our journey's over
And our Deliverer we do see
To discuss all our doings
And the pleasures we've received,
We know we shall be Home
Where love flows freely for all,
That each of us has given our best
And no effort has been too small.

SO, TO SUM UP . . .
'HEALING is not necessarily touching. It can be just sitting and talking to people, or helping someone who is disabled to be able to lead as normal a life as possible. It can be listening, counselling, encouraging and supporting.

It is the passing of Spiritual love from one person to another. All these are forms of Healing from which everyone can benefit but keep it simple.

SIMPLICITY AND TRUTH ARE YOUR WATCHWORDS.'

AN INTRODUCTION TO THE DEVELOPMENT CIRCLE

As time passed a growth in the understanding of Spiritual awareness developed. This is the story of that development.

WHEN A FEW PEOPLE ARE GATHERED TOGETHER

MEDITATION

'At times when we are alone with our thoughts and all outside influences are excluded we are at one with Spirit, learning new things about ourselves in past and present times.

These, though not readily in everyday thoughts are happenings which have moulded our lives throughout each term we have spent in whichever time, space or dimension we have needed to be to learn a new experience.

The Spirit is full of very rich experiences, all gathered over the lengthy distance of time eternal.'

THE DEVELOPMENT CIRCLE

Ursula Brown was my first Spirit contact and I got to know her really well. She was eight years old when she was crossing a road and came into collision with a bus. Her short life on the earth ended at that point.

I felt at the time it was very meaningful that my first contact should have been a child. Having taught Infants and Juniors during most of my teaching career I could relate to her. I was new to Spirit communication, and attunement in this sense of the word held a new meaning within my vocabulary.

I was just learning that Spirit vibrations are faster than ours and that to be able to communicate with us it was necessary for adjustments to be made. I felt that Ursula was learning to communicate with me and I was certainly in my infancy as regards communication with her. We were learning together to develop a perfect partnership.

During 1994 I was invited to join a Mediumship Development Circle. This was another new experience for me and I felt very inadequate when I realised how little I knew about such things.

In May of that year the writings and artwork had begun and I found a different form of Mediumship developing from that of the other Circle members.

Then I was invited to take my pad and pen with me for two meetings to see whether messages and drawings would be given to me during the second meditation.

This was at the time when Ursula was my Spirit contact and my artist helper was her Uncle William. At the first Circle I found that they were there with me too and as this proved to be a useful exercise it was extended indefinitely.

My weekly contact with Ursula also continued outside the Circle and on these occasions I was also receiving guidance which would lead me to a deeper understanding of the ways in which Spirit made contact with us and of how I would be expected to pass their messages on to others.

During the months following my invitation to join that Circle the following show the kinds of written advice I was receiving.

'You are understanding now that the thoughts in your head are communications from the Spirit World. We are guiding you in that way. It is not the way you expected is it? But you are getting used to it now.'

'In tomorrow's Circle you must do as you are doing now and write what thoughts come into your mind. We will guide you.'

'It is a good idea to photocopy the designs and give those copies to the people present so that they can look at them often, and see more in them each time they look at them.'

The peace and tranquility of the everglades brings reminiscences of times when we are alone with our thoughts and all outside influences are excluded. At this time we are at one with Spirit, learning new things about our-selves in past and present times.

These, though not readily in every-day thoughts, are happenings which have moulded our lives throughout each term we have spent in whichever time, space or dimension we have needed to be to learn a new experience.

The Spirit is full of very rich experiences, all gathered over the lengthy distance of time eternal.

'Uncle William and I will be with you at Circle tomorrow and will give you messages. We always come to Circle with you. You will know it is me because I shall blow gently at the right side of your top lip.'

'Your drawing is coming on well. Uncle William is pleased with your progress. It is right that you should do your writing and drawings in the Circle. We are all there to help you. Because there are so many of us you will find that you progress much more quickly.'

'Your Development Circle will be a small group tomorrow but we shall be with you and your Spiritual unfoldment will develop. You sometimes think that it doesn't, but we are always with you guiding you along the Spiritual pathway.'

* * * *

The group messages which I received during the second meditation are included later in this section, some with appropriate illustrations. As well as these it became a routine that I was also given messages for other participants, which I wrote down and passed on.

One member said to me recently, "I keep them all together and when I am feeling under the weather I take them out and read them. I get a lot of comfort from them. They're wonderful."

I hope that you, the reader, will gain comfort from reading them too. They are the word of my Spirit Contacts and as you read I am sure that you will find mentioned similar circumstances to some in which you have found yourselves at sometime in the past, and you will then wish, as I have done, that the relevant message had been available at that time – for understanding and guidance.

* * * *

'You will come to Mediumship through Healing' I had been told and since then I have sat in Development Circles trying to master the technique of understanding how to pass verbally to others the messages received from Spirit. It was something which I found difficult to understand.

To receive thoughts in my head which I could write down immediately was no problem. Having committed them to paper meant they required no memory retention before passing them on, and that they were delivered accurately. Also I enjoyed the surprise when reading them again later and noting not only the content but the way in which the messages within these words were expressed. They were concise, to the point, full of expression and always positive in outlook. It was explained that if a spoken word from spirit could not be 'heard' then symbols would be used and each could be interpreted to give meaning to the receiver of that particular message, and I was given an example.

"I can see a dog with you. He is sitting beside you and is very close to you. This tells me that a very good friend will be coming to see you quite soon," said the Medium and it always happened. She then explained, "I love dogs. They are such friendly animals so I always get good vibes when I am shown one. And there is also other information you can read from it, from the dog's colour, how far it is away from you, on which side of you it is (on the right for the future and the left in the past) its size, and so on." So I tried to remember all of this for when I was given the symbol of a dog. But it didn't seem to work for me.

We always had dogs at home when I was a child but after marriage it didn't seem fair to leave a dog all day on its own whilst we were both out at work. Later we did have a cat and our sons went through the usual stages of rabbits, guinea pigs, hamsters etc.

I don't dislike dogs myself but my rapport with them now is one of caution. I have been snapped at on more than one occasion so the complete trust I had as a child has partially gone. Maybe that was the reason.

"Spirit will give you a symbol which will be meaningful to you and to which you will relate." I was told, as of course the dog had been a recognisable symbol to that particular Medium.

My biggest problem however was not to recognise the symbol, it was how to interpret it so that it made sense to the person for whom it was meant and how then to pass on the accompanying message verbally. It has taken me three years to feel confident when doing so.

During that time I was advised to draw each symbol and write the meaning against it. This I did but each time someone mentioned a symbol I realised that each participant of the Circle had a different interpretation for it.

I bought a book describing the meanings of symbols. That didn't seem to help my understanding, in fact it would be fairer to say that it caused even greater confusion, because it implied that each symbol would convey the same meaning on each occasion and I had already found that not to be the case.

Then I bought some cards and drew the shape on each expecting to be able to write each different meaning for that particular symbol so that I would have a choice. Needless to say that didn't work either.

"You will be told", was a frequent explanation I heard, but who was to tell me – and how? Looking back there seemed to be an assumption that I would automatically know.

On the Circle night that it all slotted into place the symbols given to me were colours, a different one for each person present. As usual we were told to ask for more information from Spirit in order to develop the message so that each would understand.

COLOURS AS SYMBOLS

Information which Spirit has given to me when using colours as symbols include the following:–

WHITE

White to me conveys purity. It is made up of all the colours in the spectrum and enfolds all spiritual qualities. It also reminds me of snow and of skis gliding along on it, so smoothly.

My message on this occasion was –

You have a very Spiritual future and will glide along your pathway as smoothly as skis on the snow. There will be no obstacles in the way.

RED

Red is a strong colour and can imply aggression, so think before you act and use it wisely. If you need to put a point across to someone, do it kindly and with thought as to how it may be received. Ask Spirit for help if you feel you need it and the correct way will be made known to you.

Depending on its shade RED can also go towards PINK which indicates Love and here you would find a gentler application to be necessary.

ORANGE

Orange = Yellow + Red

Yellow is spiritual wisdom and Red is strength. In this case the message was strength of purpose to pursue your Spiritual work in a very wise manner.

Orange also can imply Healing both given and received. Keep up the healing you give to others but don't forget that you also need some for yourself.

You cannot give to others all the time without replenishing your own energy. So take care and make sure you top up your own energy levels too by keeping yourself well grounded.

YELLOW

Yellow is the colour of wisdom, also the colour of the sun and tells me that while surrounded with this you will receive that kind of energy to help in your work and the ability to cheer the recipient and encourage positive thoughts.

This work you will do wisely as you have many loving thoughts to pass on to others – and love passed out is also love returned, so you will both benefit.

GREEN

Green to me is the colour of Nature, of a love for plants and all growing things. Without animals, insects and reptiles living among the plants and being shielded by them, also providing homes and food for them, our countryside would be a boring and unimaginative place.

Green implies a love of nature and of all plants and creatures therein. There is a balance here and a feeling of fairness in everything which needs consideration.

'Think before you speak' could be a motto here. Balance all things in your heart before coming to a decision as to the wisest way to act.'

BLUE

Blue is for communications. On one occasion I saw a blue cornflower and the petals seemed to be exaggerated. These are pronged and they point outwards from the centre of the flower.

This lady had just begun to receive philosophical communications during the second meditation in Circle and the message given to me for her was that she would be finding that she would be able to write down these messages and that she was to keep them together. Then when the opportunity arose she should spread the news contained in them to those who wanted to listen. And as the cornflower petal points in several different directions, so Spirit's word will be spread in many unexpected ways.

I went on to advise her that if she found in the future that she was talking to a group of people, whether small or large, there would always be someone there who had come especially to receive the information which she had to give.

Spirit was giving that information to me as I spoke. That is the way Spirit works.

INDIGO

Indigo is a very strong colour, a mixture of brown and blue. Deep thought, concentration and a need to make the right choice. A very strong person with very high personal standards, who dislikes shoddiness in others.

This person sets himself a very high standard in everything he has to do.

VIOLET

Violet is a very spiritual colour signifying a compassionate person who can communicate well with others, so settling a troubled mind in another person.

When giving Healing this colour will help to start the process whereby the body can then begin to heal itself.

This brings in strength of character, compassion for others and calm behaviour allowing trust between those concerned.

PINK

Pink is the colour of love and caring. It calms the troubled and helps any problem to be brought into perspective.

A 'pink' person will be a dedicated carer of others giving love, time and all kinds of help to improve that person's situation and so encourage a more positive attitude towards the future.

BEIGE

Beige to me is made up of brown and white.

The brown is the earth and I can see you sitting in a glade in a wood with all the small woodland animals sitting around you. You send your love to all living things no matter what shape or size. In this position you are well-grounded and safe from all negativity.

The white is a strong colour which, when mixed with brown to become beige is powerful enough to lessen the strength of the darker colour.

You too are strong. You know the direction of your pathway and will not falter.

BLACK

Black would imply to me a sadness around, a necessity for upliftment. Much love and patience is required, then guidance to help the person retread a pathway which would bring him back to a point where he could then change direction. A need to stop, to stand still whilst considering where things went wrong – and after that to begin again towards a more positive future.

Sometimes this can be a very difficult task which calls for qualities of patience and tact.

GREY

Grey is black and white mixed together – a coming out of blackness towards a normal life again.

Lots of patience is needed, praise for small positive achievements and encouragement to build on each to regain that which has been lost.

Grey is the beginning of a return from darkness and should be the start of a pathway full of hope.

OBSERVATIONS

These are the definitions of colours which Spirit has given to me to form a basis of guidance for the person concerned. It must of course be realised that messages for 2 different people who are given the same colour would not necessarily be identical.

The individual person's lifestyle and character, his personal interests and many other points will be taken into consideration. So these are only guidelines and when interpretation is necessary that is between you, Spirit and the person concerned and what you pass to that person will be Spirits' message for that individual at that time – that which is right for him to know and understand, and for no one else.

Listen to Spirit as you are shown your symbol. Spirit will define its meaning at that time and there is no need for anyone to feel as worried as I have done in the past.

* * * *

The following poem was given to me by Spirit and it seems appropriate to include it at this point.

COLOURS IN NATURE

'RED sky at night, shepherd's delight.'
As the old superstition does go.
With SCARLET light in the sky so bright
Happy thoughts will surely flow.

The YELLOW sun on the following day
Cheers the wanderer on his way home.
The daffodils dance and the primroses play
As the summer days now come.

GREEN grasses and trees in the meadows and fields
Grow proudly for all to see.
The insects and birds in the hedges so lush
Congregate happily.

BLUE summer sky backing WHITE fluffy clouds
Brilliant and dazzling and fair.
Encourages the flowers in their colourful sheens
To bloom in the fresh country air.

PURPLE violets grow in the woodlands
With bluebells and primroses too.
SILVER droplets of rain are beginning to fall
And will sparkle with the dew.

ORANGE and INDIGO berries,
And those that are GREEN and RED.
Provide food for the birds and seeds to produce
More plants in the years ahead.

In the gardens we see that each thing that grows
Has a COLOUR of its own.
GOD'S purpose has been to make each one seen
And give pleasure to EVERYONE.

GUIDANCE

THE SPIRITUAL BEING

'The spiritual being is one who loves unselfishly all his fellow beings. This is what you must aspire to do. It is a very difficult task but love given is love returned, and returned many fold with blessings also from the Spirit World.

Do your best. Each time you try the task becomes easier and the end result becomes closer to completion. You are all well along the road. The end is in sight. You are on level ground now. You will find the effort worthwhile.'

HERE AND THERE

'God is here. His light does shine
On your Circle developing fine.
We're with you all, helping all we can,
To increase awareness in your fellow man.

Go out into the world and spread the news to help others understand that life continues into other worlds. We are just passing through today, stopping and learning as we do so.

Be grateful, gracious and scatter what you gather to all the ends of the earth – for all to know.'

The Circles to which I have belonged all seemed to close down during the summer and restart later in the year, sometimes with a few new faces to replace those members who had left the area.

Included here are writings which I continued to receive during the second meditation in the Circles I attended.

AN INTRODUCTION TO CIRCLE

'The pathway to divine judgement is long and straight. Go ahead with confidence and know that we are with you, leading you along the way to truth and spiritual growth.

You are here tonight to blend together as one group knowing the time is near for all to go forward. Your journeys will be smooth and you will find that all you need to know will become known to you when the time is right and it will be acceptable to you. Go forward. Spread our word. Blessings to you all.'

THE PATHWAY

'We walk along the pathway towards a better understanding of our higher selves. Our trust in Spirit and each other grows as we travel, holding our heads up high and knowing all will be well.

Along the way we shall meet rocky grounds and mishaps may occur but be positive, have faith and all will be well. The smooth path will be again in front of you and the wisdom you have gained will be your reward.'

This advice was reinforced later by –

THE WATERS OF LIFE

'The waters of life flow smoothly and all is calm. Occasionally we falter and need to take a diversion, but that need not be a negative thing.

All of these are learning experiences and if we can think back to the point where hope seemed to fail, and retrace those steps, we can know that all is well and we can go ahead, having benefitted by that experience.

Never despair. Stay calm and a new easier way will become obvious, and you will find yourself again in calmer waters.'

ENCOURAGEMENT

'Into your thoughts tonight we bring a spiritual awareness of looking forward into the future – a life full of understanding and knowing that all will be well.

Go ahead with faith in us and love in your hearts for your fellow beings. Remember that

LOVE CONQUERS OVER ALL ADVERSITY.

A positive attitude to all things smoothes out what could be a very stony pathway and life will be so much easier to bear.'

SILENCE

In the silence of our thoughts we know that GOD IS LOVE, that all good things come from Him to each and every one of us. We receive help and guidance, truth and understanding, to pass on to our fellow beings.

LISTEN to these thoughts,
UNDERSTAND what you hear – and
KNOW that it is the TRUTH.'

THE SMELL OF A PIPE

'The smoke that you smelt tells you your father is with you guiding you as you progress through the Spiritual learning that is enhancing your life. Your loved ones bid you welcome at this circle tonight and offer love and blessings to you all.

Stay together. We will give you guidance along your respective pathways. You may find the odd patch of stony ground but you will not stumble. You will be supported as you travel along.

Go straight ahead. You will achieve your goal. Satisfaction is assured for you all.'

WHERE LOVE ABOUNDS

'The island where love abounds is the one on which you will be welcomed.

Love is a boundless thing which enhances each one's life whether given or received. It, like a smile, costs nothing and can soften the hardest heart, making relaxing moments become the beginning of a Healing process.

Something so little, which costs nothing at all, can grow into an overwhelming feeling of enhancement and be the beginnings of preparation for a new awareness of the development which you are hoping for yourselves.'

THE POWER OF SUGGESTION

'The experience we shall share is one of love and happiness on an island below the sea, where life is abundant but in no way resembles that which we know.

Colours are enhanced, bright and powerful hues. Lines are meaningful and can adapt to any requirement deemed to be necessary for use or comfort.

Thought is all that is required to understand fully any experience you ask for – anything you feel you need to make your stay more comfortable. It is like Heaven on Earth. No power of suggestion cannot be met. Would you be happy in such a place?'

SPIRITUAL UPLIFTMENT

[At this Circle there were only three members present. Spirit showed their gratitude in this way.]

FLOWERS FROM SPIRIT

'Flowers from Spirit to you all this afternoon. Blessings to you all.

Thank you for doing our work and travelling along our pathways. We are always with you. You only need to ask and we are there to help you all we can to achieve a truly deep Spiritual awareness.'

WE ARE ALWAYS WITH YOU

'Sometimes you feel very alone, but you can always call on us for help. That is what we are here for. We watch over you and care for you. You are special to us and we shall ensure that you tread the pathway of life which benefits you, so that you will develop to a higher Spiritual level.

Continue to spread love around. It will be returned to you.'

PEACE

'The peace and tranquillity symbolised by the swan is with you all in your Meditation today.

Blessings to you all. As you go deeply under the sea with the dolphins so you will enjoy the calmness and wonder of the situation.

Peace be with you. Our love is with you always.'

GUIDANCE

'Hear the word of the Lord. Harken to what he says. Abide by His word and you will be guided by that wisdom. You will know the correct pathway to a peaceful co-existence. Love will be all around you and there will be friendships abounding. The world will know a new peace.

Stay calm and everything will work out and go smoothly. Patience is the password. Take things one at a time.'

TOLERANCE

'Your tolerance levels will be heightened. That does not come easily. You must work at it. With the pressures of your everyday life it is a difficult task but a very worthwhile one.

Be patient. You will reach your goal in the end.'

THE LIGHT OF LOVE

'Spread the Light of Love and you will change the way of friends and acquaintances. This, in turn, will lead others to feel good and love will spread and multiply.'

THE LIGHT FROM WITHIN US

'The light from within us shines out on to the world, helping those in need and bringing joy into the hearts of others. The light, love and peace from Spirit has entered our lives and filled us with happiness which we pass on to all we meet.

Our pathways are bright,
Our hearts are light,
And God and His Angels
Are always in sight.

Be aware of this always and go forward with trust in all that you do. All will be well. You will be safe.'

TIMES OF STRESS

'Worries and how to cope with them are all part of the training for life. We must know how to cope in times of stress and there are many such times yet to come.

Your training is going well. Spread love around you and you will be rewarded with love.'

WITH LOVE IN YOUR HEARTS . . .

'With love in your hearts you will dwell on the earth. You will be endowed with love and understanding towards your fellow beings. The tranquillity and generosity of feeling you exude will be felt by all you meet.

Go your separate ways and do God's work. We shall all meet up at the end of our journeys. God Bless you all.'

THE LANTERNED BRIDGE

'From here, across the lanterned bridge to the Castle of Enchantment, a life full of joy and wonder. A journey of happiness coming from within and radiating out to all you meet. The animals, the birds, they join in with their songs, recognising our greetings of love. For without love we are nothing. Love embraces all things and is returned in many different ways to the giver.'

THE WALLED GARDEN

'The walled garden brings security to all who enter. It is full of love, of peace and an understanding of all that is yet to come. We feel at ease with those making this journey with us. Their thoughts of love shine out to all.

Be brave, be true and know your God. You will be safe and all will be well.

Come to this garden when you need a calm, quiet and peaceful time. Think through your thoughts and know that we care. You will go away refreshed.'

NATURE

THE COMING OF SPRING

The skies are blue. The hills are green.
The winter's coming. The harvest is in.

The fields are ploughed. Mice hunt for grain.
Their search for food is all in vain.

The leaves change colour. Soon they will fall.
The snow will come encompassing all.

Some animals will sleep the whole winter through,
Then wake up to sunshine. The world will be new;

All fresh in appearance. They'll hurry around
Looking for nuts hidden below ground.

And new life will blossom in hedgerows and trees.
The spring and the sunshine us all do they please,

New life and energy in all to instil.
There'll be movement all over each dale and hill.

A freshness everywhere, happiness will glow
In all those we meet on earth here below.

Thank you, Dear Lord, for all that we see,
'Twas put here by you to benefit me.

An honour bestowed on each living thing
Is obvious to all at the COMING OF SPRING.

SPRINGTIME

'The awakening of the Souls of mortals at this time of the year brings new life and understanding within you all. New ideas will flow and create new understanding in areas yet to be discovered.

This is an exciting time for everyone. It will be cheerful, colourful and gay. The sunshine in your hearts will enhance the colours in your vision and the words you interpret as they penetrate your minds.

A new beginning is here and all that develops now will be a very wondrous experience.'

WATER

'Water brings peace and tranquillity into our lives. It flows and splashes its way along the stream of life touching everyone's heart as it travels. Let it touch your heart too.'

THE RAINBOW

'The wonder of the rainbow enlightens our lives. Its colours spread throughout the world giving love to one and all. It heralds a new world so clean and fresh – a new start for us all.

The golden sunshine will follow to take away our cares and make us feel good. We shall go forward to better things. Have courage and know that all will be well.'

THE SUN

'The warmth of the sun, its brightness and energy, charges us with vigour. We want to respond, to 'get up and go'. New life is given to everything around. Our batteries are recharged. We go onwards on our journey of service to those less fortunate than we. Spread the light around and enhance the lives of others also.'

DROPLETS OF WATER

'The droplets of water from the fountain contain all the colours of the spectrum and invigorate us as they splash over our bodies, giving new life and energy to each of us.

Each colour plays its part in the process to enliven us as we strive for Spiritual truths, cleansing our minds of unnecessary thoughts and planting within them seeds of purity and love for future growth.

Go on your way refreshed with new life and energy, and much love for your fellow travellers. The stones on that pathway will feel smooth and the journey will be effortless.'

COLOURS

'The Fountain of Peace brings all kinds of colour into our lives, the warmth of the yellow in our love for each other, the blues to calm us from everyday frustrations, the greens and reds give us directions when we need to decide where to go and what to do when performing our daily tasks. The silvers and golds are the ones which shine and sparkle and are most welcome.

Every one plays a part. Wear the colour for your own moods, bright colours for gaiety, paler more delicate shades for peace.

Feel good in the colours you wear and be happy. If you feel good others around you will do so as well. Spread love and merriment in this way. As you say 'Smile and the world smiles with you. ' A smile costs nothing and it is always reciprocated and passed on to someone else.

This is the cheapest therapy there is.'

See poem A Smile p. 159.

HERBS

'Herbs in our gardens fill the air with fragrance which wafts in the breeze, filling our homes and our hearts with a feeling of newness and wonder. The warmth of the sun dries the petals and leaves and the colours from its rays add joy and happiness, making them permanent in their uses towards increasing good health in our earthly lives.

Use your bodies as you use these plants. Preserve them carefully and they will serve you well.'

THE SEASHORE

This writing was inspired during a Meditation in which we walked along a beach.

'As you walk along the seashore, the freshest of air, the aroma of the salty sea, the purity of the water cleanse your souls. All your cares disappear and happiness is instilled within you.

Your bird illustrates the help you receive to conquer unforeseen problems along the way. It can see into the nooks and crevices you may fall into and guides you on to a safer level.

Your colourful jumpers raise your hearts and you travel without a care, knowing that you are taking the pathway that is right for each one of you.

A pebble taken from a beach is a reminder of a pleasant occasion – something you can call on during the odd times when you are at a low ebb.

Tread firmly in your walking boots. The sun will always shine in your hearts. God will always be with you. Have faith and courage on your rocky pathway.

The green grass is in sight. A welcome awaits you all.'

HARVEST TIME

'The harvesting of the corn brings the field mice into view among the poppies growing there too. The babies have gone to pastures anew. The nests are not needed again. The combine harvesters take the corn from the ears of wheat. But the tiny animals and insects are safe and move to other areas and environments to continue their growth and form new families.

Life is like this. We are born to learn new things necessary in the advancement of our lives. We have set-backs which we overcome. We become wiser from the lessons we so learn and advance our knowledge for the benefit of ourselves and others.'

Spread the information to others so that they may benefit also.'

THE CHRISTMAS TREE

'The Christmas tree brings love, jollity and merriment into our lives at the time of the year when our hearts turn to thoughts of the Christ Child, the Son of God. A time to forgive others their transgressions and make efforts to live in harmony and peace together – a mammoth task, but one which can be accomplished if everyone spreads Love and Light out worldwide this Christmas.

This can be done if we all make the effort.'

PRAYERS FOR CIRCLE

These prayers were given to me during my times of Spiritually inspired writing.

Dear Lord

Help us to grow more spiritually within this Circle today as we give ourselves to Spirit. Teach us to listen to our inner selves and to have faith in what is given to us to interpret for others.

Be with us all as we take part and encourage us to understand all that we see and hear.

Let us know that what we receive is the truth and help us to pass it correctly on to the one for whom it is meant.

Our thanks we send to Spirit.

God Bless you all.

AMEN.

Dear Loving Father

Be with us in our Circle tonight and guide us through our Meditation so that we gain an insight into all that you desire for us to know.

Bring forward the awareness of Spirit which we aim to achieve so that we can have a closer communication with you.

Help us to be patient and calm in all that we do; able to understand other people's ways, and through this to relieve the stress with which they live and with which they are trying to come to terms.

Guide us along the pathway where we learn all negative acts are learning experiences. Show us how to turn each into a positive action which will benefit the world in which we live.

And when we feel low in spirits, or are ill, please give to us your healing energies so that we can be fit and well enough to pass them on to those more needy, than ourselves. Thank you Loving Father for your help and guidance.

AMEN.

O Loving Father
  Please help us to know which way to go
  In all that we do, Dear Lord for you.
  Our lives we commend to you, our Dear Friend.
  Our pathways you know. Please help us to grow.
  Be with us today and show us the way –

Then –

  Guide each of us through
  This service to you.
  AMEN.

OR

  Please help us to know
  Which way to go
  In all that we do
  Dear LORD for you.

  A bright light does shine
  On this pathway of Thine,
  To show us the way.
  It gladdens our day.

  Please help us to stay
  On this Heavenly way,
  With a heart full of love
  Sent from above.

  For then happy we'll be
  In all we can see
  Knowing our FATHER, so dear,
  Will always be near.
  AMEN.

A NEW DAY

  Today is here – another day
  With exciting things to do.
  A good night's sleep has ensured
  Our energy is renewed.

In this fresh new world the sun will shine
And fill us all with glee.
We'll 'get-up-and-go' and so fulfil
All that is meant to be.

We have to shop and work and play,
Some things that must be done.
We pledge to help each other and
There'll still be time for fun.

We also have this commitment
To help others less able than we
Who still are blessed, with strength to serve
Our extended family.

Thank you Lord for this new day
For making us feel so good
And willing to do for other folk
What we know we really should.

Your love and guidance we all know
Keep us safely on our way.
Thus, following YOUR FOOTSTEPS we will be sure
Of a very rewarding day.
AMEN.

AT THE END OF THE DAY

Thank you, Heavenly Father,
It's been a lovely day.
I've completed many tasks
All in a leisurely way.

Each one was a real pleasure
And as it slowly unwound,
Some help from you I detected.
I felt your Angels around.

Guiding and advising me
To do next what was best
To complete each section of the act
Before putting it to the test.

And everything seemed so easy.
Your way worked out well.
You always know what is right.
I can always tell.

For you are ever with me
And always there to show
The correct way on my pathway
Along which I should go.

And when I spare time to listen,
I hear your patient voice
Suggesting and wisely helping me
To make the perfect choice.

Thank you Dear Lord for helping me
I just wanted you to know
How grateful I am for all that you do
And that I love you so.
AMEN.

THE DEVELOPMENT OF PSYCHIC ART

THE BEGINNINGS

It was in May 1994 that an exciting new happening occurred in my life. Spirit made direct contact and writings and drawings have since developed in a most interesting way.

On the evening of the 23rd I was counting the cash I had collected as Treasurer of the Northamptonshire UFO Research Club (NUFORC) making sure that it tallied with the number of people who had attended the meeting that afternoon. Each adult had paid the usual admission fee and children were admitted free.

That night I felt very particular. I had counted the adult names on the list and checked them against the money in my tin. Everything was correct. Then for some reason which I can't explain I looked again at the list. There was something there which did not appear to be right. I rechecked the numbers and the money. Nothing was wrong there – so what could it be?

I looked at the names again. They were all right. Then my eyes strayed to the bottom line where I had added two children – and there it was. I had written '2 chn'.

So what is wrong with that you probably think. Nothing now-a-days, but I went to school at the time when all abbreviated words had to have a dot at the end to show they had been shortened and not mis-spelt. Yes, I could see it now. the full-stop was missing.

The silly part of it all was that the piece of paper with the list on would be put in the litter bin afterwards anyway, but such had been my childhood education that here I was at 65 being concerned that, to me, '2 chn' without the dot was incorrect. To rectify it became a matter of high priority and I found at that moment that it had become necessary not just to write a dot there – but to emphasise the fact until it was quite obvious.

Then a strange thing happened. It was as if my pen had come to life. It was moving along the line, forwards and backwards, and up and down. Wherever my pen went my hand went too. They seemed to have a mind of their own.

About three years before this I had been able to do what had been described to me as 'automatic' writing. This was under the guidance of a healer friend, but after about a month the writings had told me to stop, and that I would know when I was to start again. So was this now the right time, I wondered.

By this time I was also a member of a Mediumship Development Circle and was therefore aware that Spirit needed a voice to link with, also that to receive more information I must ask questions – so I did.

I suggested that we should draw a yacht to see if that was the intention. I could even do that on my own, without Spiritual guidance, if that was what was happening. After all, a yacht (the way I draw it) is all straight lines. We did draw a recognisable yacht but I felt in my heart that it was mostly my work. Then I knew we needed another boat in the water I had added myself.

In what seemed to be forwards and backwards scribble I could detect a rowing boat. Then suddenly without any thought on my part, my pen shot upwards and back down and an oarsman sat in that boat. The pen then shot equally quickly down and up again at an angle and there he was, sitting rowing his boat with an oar in his left hand.

It was like magic and seemed so easy. I put some waves in the water and clouds in the sky, but I shall never forget that wonderful sensation when producing the rowing boat with its oarsman.

I didn't want to stop so I drew a tree and some bushes on a hillside, and felt there needed to be sheep there too. Suddenly it was done in the same way as the boat had been, but not by me. So I tried another animal in front of that one. I thought it was another sheep but many people think it's a bison. Anyway, I know that the only part I played in its production was to hold the pen and the pen appeared to draw the animal by itself.

After that I felt I had to draw a man or woman's head. Perhaps I was destined to be a Psychic Artist? At least it was recognisable as a face, but whose? It was to be several months later when I saw a war film on television. Playing a part in it was Anthony Quayle and I recognised the face in my 'portrait'.

After this very rewarding evening I allowed the pen more freedom to move by relaxing my hold of it. It moved forwards and backwards, up and down, and at all angles. It seemed to have a purpose when doing so and when patterns were formed I was not controlling the direction of the lines. The pen did that. When I

asked for something with meaning the patterns followed lines on the paper, as I had taught small children to do when teaching them to write. But here, at this time, it was as if it was I who was the one being taught.

We seemed to have an understanding and soon I felt confident enough to ask for a legible message. The result of this was that the pattern shapes changed into written words and I was able to have a comprehensible 'conversation' between Spirit and myself.

URSULA – THE CHILD SPIRIT

'With my mummy and daddy up in Heaven' were the first legible words I read, so I asked for more information and found that my message was from a little girl named Ursula Brown who was eight years old. She was pleased to see me and asked if I would 'play with her at writing' and I agreed.

I learnt that she had lived in Liverpool and had been a happy child when she was on the earth with her brother and twin sisters, but she had been run over by a bus when she was trying to cross the road.

She was taken to hospital where everyone was very kind to her but she could not be saved as she was 'too badly injured in the head'. Her brother and sisters were very sad when she died, but she said she is very happy in Heaven and she watches them all the time to see what they get up to – and she often has a good laugh at some of their antics.

She told me that she was in Heaven with her Mummy and Daddy, also her Grandma and Granddad. She described the coloured flowers there, also the Angels and God who loves everybody. "And he loves you too" she told me.

Some of my friends wondered why my first contact with the Spirit World should be with a child. I felt it was very appropriate. I had spent many years as a teacher of young children. I had likened the 'scribbles' to writing patterns taught to those children when learning to write. Also I was new to this kind of communication and I felt that she was too. I was certain that in time we would grow to become very close partners in this exercise. It was an exciting prospect and I hoped it would continue.

URSULA'S WORLD

One of the first pieces of information I received from Ursula was about her world. "I want to tell you about heaven," she wrote.

"It is lovely here. We have plenty to keep us busy. I help to look after the children. Many come here when they are very small. I am happy helping them to get used to being here. If they are poorly when they come, they are made well. You only have to think of yourself as being well and you are better again. We learn many Spiritual things and grow in Spiritual strength. I shall tell you about these things when I write again."

Then –

'In the Spirit world there are many ways to go on a journey. You can go to the level when you are coming in, or you can go to a lower level and work upwards. As you progress you go to a higher level. You make the progress in an awareness of the Spirit to be a much better balanced Spirit, then you reach a new Spiritual level. I can see that you will want to develop yourself. If you will help the ones on a lower level to raise themselves up they will then be wiser and rise upwards.'

'If you can break the habit of a lifetime and have an open mind', she assured me, 'you will find that you will receive much wisdom of learning. I hope you will harken to my words. Listen to your inner self. Trust your first impressions. We will help you to interpret and understand what we give you and you will do well.'

I wasn't sure that I understood all of that. I felt there was a tremendous amount for me to learn, but later in another message I was to realise that it would not be too difficult a task.

'You are understanding now that the thoughts in your head are communications from the Spirit world.' I was told. 'We are guiding you in that way. It is not the way you expected, is it? But you are getting used to it now.' And I was. Information about my world was to follow soon afterwards.

'Tonight I will tell you about the World as we see it,' was written. 'There is a lot of turmoil on your planet. We can see both good and bad influences at work. You will find yourself working towards eradicating these evil influences as time passes. There is a lot to do.'

I was preparing to attend a course on Psychic Art at the Arthur Findlay College in Stansted Hall the following week and was told that there I would find others like me who will all be wishing to help to bring love and concord into the lives of those who have gone astray.

'To find one lost sheep and return it to the fold is a happy occasion,' Ursula continued, 'and you will experience this. But there is so much to do. So many are going astray now. Do your best to bring them home again.'

WILLIAM BROWN

I was soon to find that Ursula was not my only contact. What had seemed to be uncontrolled patterns were to change and become meaningful coloured designs and I was to find that it was Ursula's Uncle, William Brown, who was guiding me at this point.

'My uncle will help you to draw patterns and designs, and in time he will guide you into the way of a Psychic Artist. You will enjoy doing that, I am not very good at drawing things myself. I know you enjoy drawing patterns but you don't remember detail. You will have to have faith in us and we will do it for you. You should hold your pen loosely so that the writing or drawing can flow easily as the pen is moved. Don't press on it at all' was the advice.

An artistic element seemed to be creeping into the relationship and I wondered why.

'I wanted to help you to understand how easy it is to have contact with the Spirit World.

You must put your faith in us and follow your inner feelings, then you will always do what is the right thing.'

Then the patterns changed and we drew a swan, which was to become a very appropriate symbol to which I could relate.

'The SWAN is a graceful bird and means a lot to you. It will be a symbol you will be able to relate to.

It shows you are a very Spiritual Soul and like the swans you and John will be together for life, but you have always known that haven't you?

WHITE SWAN is your Guide and Helper and you have seen his influence in your drawings.

WHITE SWAN was a North American Indian and his tribe watched over and revered the Silver Trumpeting Swans, now unfortunately near extinction. If you can find a picture of one you will see that they have a special beauty and you will understand why you are drawn to them?'

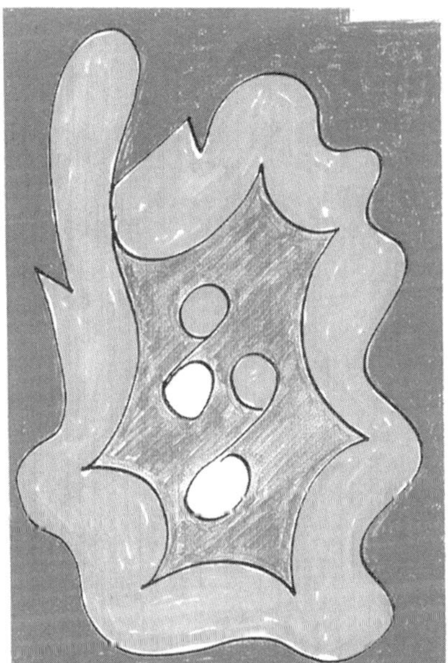

MARY JENKINS

A dot on an abbreviated word (chn. children) started my arm shaking and had resulted in contact with Ursula from whom I received Spirit messages; from her Uncle William Brown, who guided me into the world of Psychic Art and encouraged the control of my hand when drawing patterns and designs, also the swans.

At the beginning of Sept. 94. William, who had taught me the basics, wrote that he would be moving on to help another would-be Psychic Artist and that I would be getting a new teacher.

By this time Mary Maceachrane, whose Mediumship Development Circle I had joined, was impressed with what I was doing and suggested that I should do writings and drawings during the second meditation at Circle.

At the next meeting my new Spirit teacher, Mary Jenkins was with me. She further developed the hand control which William had started, and during her time with me I was able to join others at Stansted Hall, the Arthur Findlay College, for tuition in Psychic Art from Coral Polge.

My week there introduced me to Psychic Portraits, Auragraphs, and Platform Mediumship to a lesser degree, and was a week full of surprises.

We had to take with us samples of our artwork and talk about it to the rest of the group. I was very new to this but did my best. After showing them my drawings etc. from William and Mary, and saying that I thought the SWAN had a significance for me, a lady in the group who I only knew as 'Mary' told me that she collected swans and had many in her collection. She had made a study of Egyptian Symbols and she gave me some advice regarding their meanings. Also she said that her name used to be Mary Jenkins.

The following day a young man named John told me that he was studying the North American Indian Medicine Cards and that he had just got to the Swan. He allowed me to study that information.

On the final day the Psychic Artists linked up with the mediums.

We had to draw a Psychic Portrait for one of them – and talk about it publicly – what a shock!

However, with the help of my inspired writing and thoughts, also my pendulum, I got the correct information and my young sailor from Portsmouth was recognised.

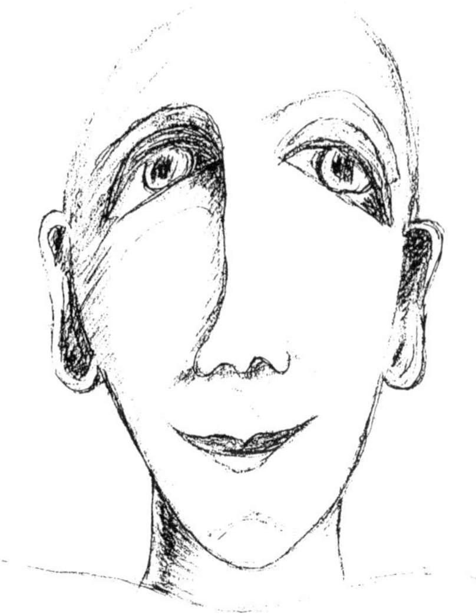

Then followed more feminine designs and some very colourful patterns from Mary Jenkins into which I was also able to read messages.

These continued for a while but gradually the drawing changed. It was developing into designs which were done with a Pilot Drawing Pen No. 8 and filled in laboriously with the same pen, a process which took around two hours to complete. But here the hand control came into its own and as time passed the filling in of the shapes was almost halved.

These designs were a different style from Mary Jenkins's and I began to wonder whether she had gone on, like William Brown to help another aspiring artist on the next stage of progression. She hadn't said, but it did seem then that I could possibly be receiving advice from someone else. And having realised that things began to slot into place.

UNCLE HERBERT

I was asked by members of the Development Circle how I did the black and white drawings I had taken to show them and which were being greatly admired. I demonstrated how my hand was guided and the pen produced the design. I promised to colour it before the next Circle to show the finished effect.

Also at Circle I had explained that in the design I had done for a friend's reading there was a small section which reminded me of something I had been given after my paternal Grandmother had died; something which I had found again when looking for something else – and now again I couldn't remember where. In two recent designs I had done, a similar shape had reminded me of this too.

A few days before this I had found myself standing in the bedroom saying aloud, "Why am I here?" I opened the door of the wardrobe in front of which I stood and there at the back left-hand corner of a shelf was the object of which I had been reminded – a holder for a pen or paintbrush which had been designed and made by my Father's brother, Herbert Walter Lawson, who had died around the time of World War 1 and of course, whom I had never met.

He was the artist in the family and my brother Ted, our cousin Barry and I have over the years, inherited the many paintings which covered the walls in our Grandparents' home. I have the paint box he used, a box and tray he carved so beautifully – and this pen/paintbrush holder.

For some reason I had found myself being drawn to those things at that time.

Following this I did two designs in which this symbol also appeared. Once was a surprise, twice a co-incidence, but a third time made me sit up and take notice. Could my Uncle Herbert be my new artist helper in Spirit?

William Brown had introduced me to this new skill, giving me exercises in hand-control and bold colourful patterns; then Mary Jenkins introduced me to a more feminine type of picture and design, and the understanding of Egyptian Symbols, so encouraging me to read the messages within them.

But my type of drawings had changed again, this time to bold black and white designs and I wondered if I had progressed to the third stage of instruction – and if so, with whom?

I felt there were clues in the symbols (A, B, C, D) and found the object they reminded me of (E) but the strange thing about all of this was that having found

A

B

C

D

the actual thing of which these parts of my designs (A, B, C, D) had reminded me – they turned out in reality to be nothing like the original thing (E) at all, but I still felt I had a new helper. Could it possibly be my own Uncle? By this time I had attended Circle for about two years. At the next meeting I explained what had happened and it was readily confirmed by Spirit. My Uncle was indeed my new helper at this level of progress into Psychic Art.

Those who had followed my development along this Spiritual pathway had noticed the change and were admiring the improved standard in my work and the striking designs. If I had needed further confirmation of the identity after Circle I was to find that forthcoming too, for as I filled in the black areas of that design with my Pilot Drawing Pen No. 8 I was to see that same symbol forming again within it, but this time it was accompanied by a very strong smell of tobacco and I knew that not only was Uncle Herbert guiding my hand in the artwork, but his brother, my Father, who was rarely seen without his pipe when he was on the earth had also come along and the completion of that design became a wonderful family reunion.

The smell of pipe tobacco had become obvious to me on a previous occasion. It had been an Open Day in Church Stowe and I had visited several villagers' gardens. This was during a period when I had been inspired to do writings and poems, and that night my mind had been taken to the War Memorial, a Celtic Cross, and the seat by it. This seat had been placed there in memory of my Father, Cyril Brian Thomas Lawson.

Just after I had visited a garden near the Manor in Church Stowe I was on my way to visit the handicraft display in St Michael's Church. Suddenly there was a very strong smell of pipe tobacco. No one was in sight at that moment, but later a man appeared and as he came towards me I noticed he had a pipe in his mouth.

But – as he came nearer the strong smell of tobacco lessened, until he reached me and I could see that his pipe was not alight.

Later I was inspired to write:–

THE SMELL OF A PIPE

'The tobacco-y smell wafted through the breeze bringing memories of one long gone. One who had trodden that pathway, getting pleasure in later years from the simple things that presented themselves within the vicinity of the home in which he resided. The walks around the village, chatting over a garden gate, discussing gardening, the countryside, the animals. Standing there smoking his pipe, putting the world to rights.

Do I know such a man? Yes, it's Dad. God Bless you Dad and thank you for that memory through the smell of tobacco smoke.'

JOSEPH ELIAS

On 12th August 1996 I sensed that my drawings had changed again. They were still black and white but the symbols which had been present were now missing. I asked Spirit for confirmation and received the following information.

'You have noticed that your drawings have changed again. Your Uncle has gone forward now and you are being helped by a friend of his Joseph Elias who will be with you for a while. Your pictures will now be more of the Surrealist type and will appear to others to be more imaginative.

Each artist has his own style and you will soon get to notice a change in what you produce.

You enjoy a change of instructor and notice it very soon. Although we did not tell you your Uncle had moved on you were able to notice it yourself. It was good that your own Uncle was able to help you to develop your artwork. You have always admired his paintings since childhood. Good Luck.'

Then I asked Joseph to tell me more about himself and I received this.

'I was born in 1921 at Exeter and began to paint at quite a young age. I was a highly imaginative lad and the portrayal of ordinary everyday objects in this new way was just right for me. I did not become famous as some artists did but I enjoyed illustrating things in this special way. It gave the viewer food for thought and many recognised that there were familiar points within, as they looked deeper into them. From this type of artwork, and also literature, came an understanding to the people who searched for hope at that time when in many lives there seemed to be only despair.

I am helping you at this level of your artwork to help you to understand the deeper meanings within the work which you have been born to do. You know that life can be very complicated, but if you set aside time to look deeply into what you see and hear, a new kind of understanding will develop within you – one which will have a reward of its own and which you will be able to convey accurately and wisely to others when the time is right to do so. Good Luck.'

My writings and drawings continued in Circle and other suggestions were made there regarding the development of my artwork, pastel drawings and auragraphs being some of them.

PASTEL WORK

PASTEL WORK

The suggestion that I should do pastel drawings filled me with horror. Memories at Primary School level flooded back when during my 7–11 year age group we spent a great deal of time using them. They were the messiest things imaginable. The dust seemed to get everywhere and in those days before World War II there was no fixature for the work. My recollection of those classes was of messy fingers, drawings, desks and clothing and the thing we enjoyed most about it all was to blow the excess off the paper on to the backs of the children who sat in the rows in front of us. So the suggestion of pastel work was something which I did not accept with any enthusiasm at all.

Then I found that pastels had changed over the years so I bought a box of Oil Pastels and a sketch pad just to try them out. This in comparison was a real pleasure. There was no mess at all.

It was a phase which did not last for long as the black and white designs seemed to take prominence at that time, but I did do a few representations of flowers which gave me a certain amount of satisfaction.

PSYCHIC PORTRAITS

Every now and again it seemed that I might become a Portrait Artist. There were several attempts which were recognisable but other than the sailor at Stansted Hall, none was recognised by a friend or relative.

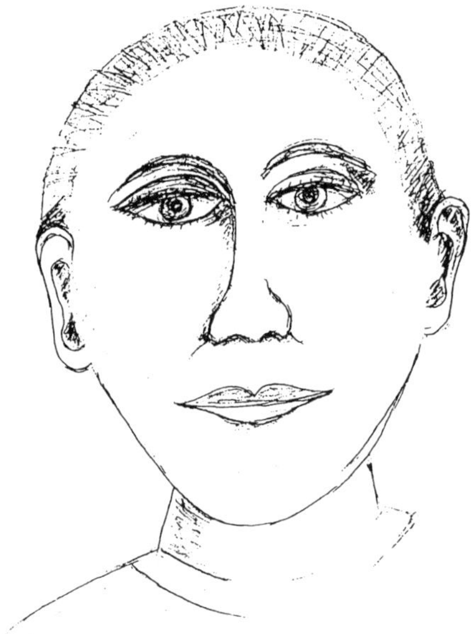

AURAGRAPHS

At one Development Circle it was given to me that I should be doing Auragraphs.

"But I don't see auras," I answered in protest.

"You don't need to. You will be told what to do and what colours to use," came a confident reply. But I was not so sure.

However, always ready for a new challenge, one evening soon after this conversation I decided to see what would happen. Just as with my Stansted sailor I asked questions of Spirit and double-checked the 'feelings' I got for my answers with my pendulum. I found that I was to do the drawing in an oval-shaped frame and use paint pencils with which to colour it.

I bought an oval-shaped cut-out from a picture framing stall on Daventry Market, drew around the shape and produced the design with a black pen. Checking the colours to use I filled in the design and when completed I was given a reading which I wrote down to accompany it.

The first one I did was for myself to prove to me that I really could do it. It turned out to be so simple and uncomplicated that I wondered why I had been so negative about it in the first place. Then followed a few for family and friends but I have not pursued them as conscientiously as I have the black-and-white designs which have always seemed to take priority and which, during the following years I was able to use in a variety of ways thanks to suggestions by members of our local Craft Class.

SPREADING THE WORD

My messages from Spirit regarding the information I receive is that it should be passed on to all who are ready to receive it and as regards the artwork I have done this in the following ways.

- Christmas and Birthday Card Covers.
- Notelets in a homemade presentation box.
- Framed pictures for presentation on special occasions – sometimes accompanied by a personal message from Spirit.

To accompany personal drawings (black and white) from Spirit I would enclose the following advice.

If you meditate on this picture you will find something within it to which you can relate and a new understanding of that point will be given to you.

Turn me around and you will see
A reminder here – of a memory,
Something of happiness maybe
In which you will find a moment of glee.
Or perhaps one of sadness you don't understand.
But be positive about it and in it you'll find
A new understanding for all that has been
And a hidden joy then can also be seen.

- Sweat-shirt and T-shirt transfers which used the same design as on the accompanying Greetings Card to personalise both card and gift.
- Individual cards using the design and a spiritual message which accompanies it.

But sometimes an extra ingredient in another form is used to enhance the greeting – A Poem.

POEMS

To complete Christmas, Birthday and Anniversary Cards, verses for each occasion were also forthcoming and these made each very special for the recipient.

Since 1994 many messages have been given to me in poetry form. Some have been very serious and others very light-hearted.

They have covered all ranges of emotions from Prayers in Circle to concerns about drug users, the changing climate, UFOs, train journeys, household chores, the angler's choice of bait, Healing etc. and some are printed where relevant in other sections of this book.

Passages of Time.

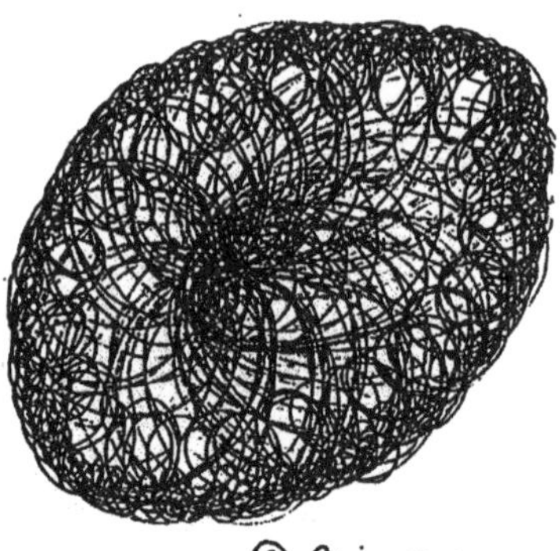

© Elsie Oakensen

This represents the world as you know it. It is covered in passages of time in all directions. Life is a passage of time, some of which is spent on one planet and some on others. We all intermingle in the universe, increasing our knowledge many ways – travelling through time and space, and resting occasionally in one place – to pass on to those there the wonderful information we collect on the way.

THE TREE

© Elsie Oakensen

The trunk of a tree represents the relationships and the root system is friendships.
When a personal relationship suffers external pressures like sickness, financial problems or whatever else – it is as when winter storms batter the tree.
Then the tree stays solid because it has this fantastic root system.

THE PSYCHIC WAY –
LEADING TO AN UNDERSTANDING OF

DOWSING

GETTING TO KNOW MY PENDULUM

Arriving home from that first Psychic Event (p. 57), my main priority seemed to be to read the instructions accompanying my pendulum. Also included was a small piece of yellow paper.

It was suggested that I should hold the pendulum above the paper and ask, "Is this paper yellow?" I did so and it swung from left to right and back again. Reading the instructions further I realised that this would be my pendulum's answer YES to any question I asked which needed that answer.

Then in a similar way as instructed I asked, "Is this paper red?" Immediately it swung in a clockwise direction. I had ascertained that the pendulum would swing sideways to answer YES to any question I asked requiring that answer and in a clockwise direction to answer NO. Then I asked several questions all requiring a YES or NO answer. I already knew the answers to these so I was able to check the accuracy of response from the pendulum. I found all the answers to be correct.

I had mastered the instructions and was ready to put the pendulum to good use. But for what? I must admit I felt very inadequate at that time. The lady on the stall had demonstrated how to use it to find the width of an aura, but as I had never seen an aura I couldn't see the relevance of that exercise.

However, I was soon to meet new people who used a pendulum regularly and my pendulum and I started on a partnership which is on-going to this day.

CHECKING THE WIDTH OF MY AURA

"Hold your pendulum by your side," the lady had said. "Now take it slowly outwards away from your body."

During this time the pendulum had hung vertically and continued to do so, then it seemed that, although my hand which held the wool was gradually moving further away, the crystal itself had become stationary and the twisted wool holding it was at an angle.

"There you are," she said, "When that happens your crystal has reached the outer edge of your aura."

But never having seen an aura I was unable to imagine what it was I was supposed to be seeing or the relevance of such an exercise. But I expected it would come in handy at some time in the future, though I could not imagine why.

THE CROP CIRCLE

In the early 1990s there seemed to be a new phenomenon happening – crop circles. I had heard them mentioned but had only seen photographs of them in magazines and newspapers.

Then, one day as I turned the pages of our local newspaper one had been reported in a corn field not too far away, and I was invited by a friend to go along to see it.

Between us we took a compass, a tape recorder, string, knife and tape-measure, a crystal and my pendulum. Having ascertained the points N, S, E and W measurements were taken of the size and all were recorded. I walked around the circle in an anticlockwise direction and recorded the feelings in my hand from the crystal, then I did the same thing using my pendulum.

At points N. S, E and W it swung in a clockwise direction denoting No, but at the centre of the circle it swung sideways for YES. Not having asked any specific questions at those points I was not able to read any relevant responses, nor have I since found anyone who has been able to explain to me why this happened.

This was an interesting exercise where curiosity was concerned but not for genuine research. Although we had not noticed any abnormal reactions in our own feelings as we conducted these exercises we later concluded that there must have been a different kind of energy within that circle, because on the way home it was obvious to me that a headache was developing. Soon afterwards I had a tightening sensation around my head, and it felt as if the top was becoming inflated like a balloon. On arriving home I became very, very tired and slept soundly for an hour and a half.

I woke up feeling elated and this euphoric state lasted from then right through to the end of the following day. Thirty-six hours after our visit we described it as 'a supportive experience in some way endorsing oneself.' We both felt we had been given something, a kind of inner strength, and agreed that often, what at the time manifests itself as a casual experience, registers later as something which has much more relevance.

I have spoken since to those whose names are linked to serious investigation into the reasons for crop circles and know that this reaction is not unique. I was delighted to have had that experience and it is one which I will not forget.

LEY-LINES

Having bought this pendulum it seemed logical when looking through the Adult Education Courses available, to find one which would help me to understand more about the direction in which I then seemed to be travelling, so I decided to join one which incorporated Crystal Healing, the Pendulum and Reflexology, if only to prove whether or not I would be interested enough to follow them on later in the year.

The first was mostly about Reflexology and it took no time at all to decide that this was not to be a subject for deeper study on my part. Crystal Healing on the other hand held more promise as I was doing Spiritual Healing and this seemed to be another aspect of it, but later it seemed to be more complicated and I opted to continue with the simpler method.

By then my pendulum had become a very good friend. I was using it a lot and found it to be very useful. Whenever in doubt about anything I could always get a second opinion!

It was on this course that I met a lady named Audrey. We had much in common where Healing, crystals and the pendulum were concerned and later worked together in a Healing group.

It was during this time that I was invited to her home, told to bring my pendulum with me and asked to use it to check some information. She wouldn't tell me what and I was set the task of finding out and reporting the different reactions I found in different areas of her garden.

Eventually having reported the 'YES' and 'NO' answers I got in different areas of her garden I was let into the mystery. I had been able to confirm what she already knew – that a Ley-line ran through her garden and under her house.

We decided to follow this further and a few days later we visited the site of an old castle just outside the village. There we dowsed with two of her neighbours to see what history we could unearth.

By then others were impressed by the information I could receive with the use of my pendulum but Audrey had much more sensitive reactions from a crystal which she held in her hand.

On that day, in our own particular ways we made many discoveries on that site, eg. the ley-line under Audrey's home also went to the castle where it crossed with another. Audrey is also very psychic and able to deduce the original use in many of the areas. Confirmation was given by my pendulum.

We found ourselves at one point standing where an altar had once been, we established that one of the ley-lines which crossed there was about 11 metres wide. We found an underground stream, and a squarish shaped field which would have been a parade ground. Then later I experienced the same feelings that I had after my visit to the crop circle. After a really good night's sleep I felt invigorated as if my batteries had been recharged.

LEY-LINES AND UFOs

After the visit to the castle I wondered whether there could be any connection between ley-lines and UFOs.

Church Stowe is in the parish of Stowe-IX-Churches which is reputed to be on a ley-line – and our village church is dedicated to St Michael. I decided that my pendulum could possibly throw some light on to this, so on a map of the area I drew a straight line from the Castle site to the point in the village where I had sat in darkness whilst circular bright lights with no beams had shone on the road around the front of my stationary car. I dowsed there and found that it was on a ley-line.

Then on the map I extended that line and found that it also crossed the road on the outskirts of the village at the point where the electrics of my car behaved irrationally.

Further interest in this exercise arose later when the line was continued. It crossed the A5 and went through Nether Heyford at a point where, on 18th August 1993 I was able to stand inside another crop circle. It was most interesting to note here that also in the field was a line of pylons and this circle was extremely close to one of them.

Following this visit I also experienced tiredness and later a feeling of elation, so it seems logical to me now to assume that there definitely is some special kind of energy within a crop circle, and that in all probability UFOs can make use of it.

OTHER USES FOR A PENDULUM

ANSWERS TO QUESTIONS

Some people find they are not able to use a pendulum. I don't know why. I have never had any problems at all with mine.

The most difficult part of the exercise had been learning how to word the questions so that they would be given a YES or NO answer, also I had to realise that if my question was long and involved it would be much easier to get a clearer result by breaking it down into shorter questions.

However with practice I would talk to the pendulum and outline my problem before I started, then I would finish up by asking, "If I split this up into small sections, can you help me find an answer please?" – and it always worked, though it would take much longer to do in that way. Often the answer to one question would lead to another which had not been on my original list but I found this to be a bonus because this way the information I received was more detailed.

DIETARY ADVICE

I also found my pendulum to be very good for Dietary Advice. Some years before this I had been diagnosed as having food allergies and to ask if I would become ill if I ate certain (named) foods became a very useful way to ensure that the migraine attacks I had suffered since the age of 12 gradually became a thing of the past.

MANAGING WITHOUT MY PENDULUM

Soon it became obvious to others that I was becoming dependent on my pendulum and it was remarked on at a meeting.

"Will you do something for me?" asked Gary one day. "Of course," I answered.

"Stop using your pendulum for 3 months," he said, "and see what happens."

That was really a shock and although I agreed I really did wonder how I would manage without it.

It didn't make a lot of difference at home because I only bought what I knew I could eat, but to do the shopping without it was something I was not looking forward to. But I had promised and I had to report back to him at the next meeting.

During the next week I stood in the supermarket looking at the interesting packaged food. I read the ingredients and by then I knew which would make me ill. The picture on the box made the contents look so tasty. I picked up one which I knew would be all right.

"Now," I said to myself as I held it, "I wonder whether I will be OK if I eat what is in here?" Suddenly my body swung to the left and then to the right with such force that it surprised not only me but a customer next to me.

"Sorry," I said rather guiltily, "I lost my balance" and we both laughed – but I knew then that I had some serious thinking to do.

The YES movements from my pendulum had transferred themselves to my body. I felt I could cope with that but what would happen about my NO answers. They were a clockwise movement and I had to test it. If that really happened I would look rather silly, I thought.

So I picked up a package of food I knew I couldn't eat, and asked myself, "If I eat this will I be ill?" Immediately the reply came. My body tilted backwards, then forwards so sharply that I nearly fell over.

"Whoops!" I said to another surprised customer "I must be drunk!" and we laughed. "Are you sure you're all right?" she added as she prepared to push her trolley away. "Yes thank you," I replied, "I just lost my balance. It's old age!" and with a knowing smile she went on her way.

I had achieved what I had hoped for. I no longer needed to be dependent on my pendulum. My own body had become one and whenever I required an answer in public all I needed to do was to ask myself a question and I gave myself the answer. Once I had recognised this I was able to control the movement of the responses.

"How are you getting on?" asked Gary the next time we met – and I told him.

"I thought you would find that would happen", he replied, and smiled confidently.

But with this experiment I had found something quite unexpected – that one of my set responses had changed viz. that for NO. On my pendulum a clockwise swing and now on my body a backwards and forwards movement. I had something new to get used to, but there was also a plus here. When standing (and it works when I am sitting down too) it is much safer to rock gently back and forward than to gyrate clockwise!

DOWSING ON A MAP

During this time I attended a most interesting course using a pendulum in conjunction with a map, the aim being to find the sites of ancient buildings in the area we were in, and this has reminded me of some dowsing which I took part in just after I became a Healer.

It was during the time of IRA bombings in this country that a group of us used maps to find possible places which could have been, at that time, being used as hide-outs for bomb-making equipment and information regarding future targets. All this was passed on confidentially to the appropriate authorities.

* * * *

Over the years which followed that Psychic Event in Daventry it was as if they became a magnet to me. I needed to go to meet new people and to learn more about myself.

I didn't understand much of what I heard but there in the privacy of a one-to-one situation I was able to ask the questions which were causing great confusion in my mind at that time. These people had so much to say and I had a need to know. It was as if I had become addicted. It was a whole new world to me.

It was also interesting to see how they worked. Most did verbal readings which were recorded on cassette. That was a relatively new system at that time and I liked it. It enabled me to listen to the information which had been given in a more leisurely moment when time allowed, and I could absorb it slowly.

I had been told that I was a Medium. Should I be able to do this kind of thing I began to wonder? But what if I got it all wrong? I felt that there would be a lot of help needed before I became as proficient as they were.

My interest was such that I visited every Psychic Event that was held locally. With friends I travelled miles and the most fascinating thing I began to notice was the many different ways this work was being done.

It wasn't just someone sitting and telling me things about myself that I didn't know. That seemed to be basically what each did, but there were such a variety of techniques and as time went by it was these that really made my visits most interesting.

"In time you will be doing this," was said many times, but my faith in me was not as strong as other people's. Still, it was time well spent and I met so many like-minded people.

I had readings, not only using ordinary playing cards, but with Tarot Cards, Runes, Crystals, numbers, handwriting, coloured stones, coloured water in small bottles, also a crystal ball. It seemed that it didn't matter what was used the information flowed freely and I wondered why.

One lady just seemed to sit and think, then wrote down messages on paper. It all seemed very strange at the time.

GUIDES AND HELPERS

Another thing which was new to me was the mention of GUIDES and HELPERS. Guides – to lead me where, I wondered? Helpers – what kind of helpers and for what?

The Psychic Artist had said she could draw a portrait of a family member or a Guide but I had recognised it as being my Grandmother so that hadn't helped me to understand what a Guide was.

I had met Charles Chapman and the Healing energies were coming through. I was also meditating whenever the opportunity presented itself, going deep within myself and closing down all outside influences. At this time there was a feeling of peace and a knowing that Spirit was very close. I was coming to terms with the fact that I was a Channel which enabled this Spiritual help to reach those who needed it. I was beginning to understand, but how much more easily I could do so if I could actually see who it was who was helping me.

My Spiritual knowledge at that time was so limited that although I always felt my dead parents to be near me, it had never occurred to me that although unseen they were still in my thoughts and so were helping me as and when it was necessary. I actually expected that someone would spell it out for me, but it was some time before I felt able to start asking questions. Then I wondered why I had not done so before because once over that hurdle everything had a meaning which I understood, and an even more relaxing and interesting existence became noticeable. There had been a reason behind my thirst for all this knowledge and I felt grateful that these new interests were becoming part of my future.

As time passed things gradually fell into place. A whole new exciting world had opened up where I would learn to recognise and accept these gifts and be meeting many new people who would be willing to pass on their knowledge to help me use them, and so understand the various ways in which contact with Spirit could be possible.

As my interests in the psychic side of things developed a regular question I was asked was, "Aren't you seeing faces yet?" It seemed to be the first thing that I should expect to happen, but it didn't seem to be working. Perhaps I was trying too hard!

Then, one night I awoke to see a bright light in the sky. It was a large orange ball with the top left-hand corner cut off. As I watched it, it descended below the horizon leaving a bright orange glow on the undersides of the cloud layers above it. Then it was no longer visible.

I returned to bed and as I turned over on to my side a large face slowly appeared in front of me. It was that of a North American Indian with lined facial features and longish grey hair.

At that time I had just begun to find myself able to receive Spiritual messages and one had told me that my Helper, when doing the Healing was a North American Indian named Mukelib.

"Mukelib, is that you," I asked, but I received no reply and the image faded away.

This, as I look back was also my first experience of clairvoyance.

* * * *

When my artwork began to develop and my Spirit Helper was William Brown he gave me pictures of swans, and it was then explained to me that White Swan, my Helper and Guide, was influencing my drawings at that time. There are also others in this development who are mentioned in more detail in the section of this book which is attributed to the development of Psychic Art (p. 107).

* * * *

The first Spirit Guide I was conscious of knowing was Ursula Brown. She introduced herself as a young girl from Liverpool.

She stayed with me, 'writing to me' weekly and introducing all the Guides and Helpers as various sections of this book unfolded.

She was with me at Development Circle and through the early years of Psychic Art and introduced me, when the time was right, to Jellicoe and Joseph on the 16th anniversary of my UFO sighting.

After my UFO encounter I had been hypnotised and during this time I described two grey forms which seemed to have life. They have always been affectionately referred to by me as 'my friendly ghost-like beings' and now here they were giving me their names and the following information, putting everything into perspective and a level of understanding which I could accept.

Ursula left soon afterwards. In the time she was with me we had both grown in knowledge, she about contact with the Earth plane and I about contact with the Spirit World. Then having completed her role in helping me to understand about the Spirit World she went off to help another aspiring Medium to reach the same level.

Jellicoe and Joseph are still with me. We have weekly contact and their guidance is very encouraging. The information I need is given to me at my own level of understanding so that I can cope with each new expectation without being overwhelmed.

All the writings for this book have been given to me by Ursula, Jellicoe and Joseph in a down-to-earth way so that they are relevant and easily understandable for us all.

The people at the Psychic Events who were giving information freely to those of us interested enough to make an appointment made me feel that they must have some inner quality which I did not understand.

They were so confident in all they said and so much of it was very accurate at the time, although I had met none of them before, and the forecasts which they made for the future had a habit of being accurate too. It all seemed very strange at the time.

CLAIRVOYANCE

To this day I believe that it was Mukelib's face which I saw (p. 137). It was explained to me that I was becoming more clairvoyant and as time passed I did see more faces. At one point I noticed that each one wore spectacles and it reminded me that it was time to have my eyes tested. It turned out to be a very timely reminder.

Then there were occasions when I saw buildings and bombs and some were followed by those same images on television news coverage at the time of the Gulf War.

Later on, platform work was being explained and demonstrated during a course I attended. When it came to my turn to participate I found I could 'see' pictures in my mind and could describe accurately detail of shape, sex, colour, animals, people etc. so that recognition was made for the acceptance of a message which I had been given.

My psychic artwork has developed through many stages and seems to be staying at present on the black and white drawings and diagrams described in the separate section on that subject (p. 107).

At one point it was suggested by a fellow sitter in Circle that a change was necessary to a different artistic medium. I was not sure.

Then I was shown black and white flowers which I drew and clairvoyantly was shown black and white cows near a well-known local churchyard.

These I took as a message to emphasise that I should continue in that way and I still do so.

A reversal of what I expected clairvoyance to be happened when I was healing a patient. I saw myself sitting to one side of her and was being shown the Healing energies flowing through me and into the patient.

"Spirit is showing you how they see you when they work through you," I was told (p. 68).

CLAIRVOYANCE means 'Clear Seeing' but to me it implies being able to see what is not visible in the normal meaning of the word.

Having now had lots of practice I would describe it in my case as being able to 'see' something in my mind which is not visible to others, but which I can describe accurately to them so that they can recognise it also.

CLAIRAUDIENCE

Similarly, what Clairvoyance is to Sight so Clairaudience is to Hearing – Clear Hearing, and as it develops within me I shall expect to 'hear' words which I shall then be able to pass on to others as and when necessary.

At present I don't think of myself as having mastered this as competently as I expect to. I assume that I should 'hear' sentences as a sound, audible to me and to no one else.

It is true that on two occasions I have been surprised when I heard my name 'called' and looking around found myself to be alone. It was 'Elsie' in the clearest tone possible, nothing at all like a human voice. It was so pure and so clear. Is this the beginning of a clairaudient conversation I wonder? I really do hope so.

But then, maybe I am misinterpreting the method of receiving the messages which are already coming to me prominently and purposefully.

All the Spiritual messages I have included elsewhere in this book have been relayed into my mind when I am relaxed and I have a pen in my hand. The words just happen to be there and the pen transfers them on to paper at my own speed – and during this time I can ask questions and receive more detail and clarification if necessary. This I have felt to be a 'thought' process.

Perhaps this could be another form of clairaudience at which I am now quite proficient, but that I have never categorised it as such. I am told that everything will come to me in my own time and at my own level of understanding. I am sure I have further to go before I feel assured about this but as with other psychic phenomena there are bound to be different aspects in each to suit the recipient. I also know that we are all tested in a variety of ways to be certain that the right medium is found so that we can be certain of the ultimate success when doing Spirit's work, which of course is to pass on accurately all information which is given by Spirit to the person for whom it is intended.

As time passes and new talents result from this training I find it all very exciting.

THOUGHT COMMUNICATION

Recently I attended a Course during which the aim was to develop a closer contact with the Spirit World, and as with all organised courses some aspects stand out as being more appropriate to the Students' needs than others.

On this course both verbal and written contact were encouraged but one specific exercise has become a very useful tool for giving me a deeper understanding of any point for which I need clarification or guidance.

It was described as a – 'Conversation with your thoughts' – and it is so easy to do. Thought comes from your inner self and unless spoken can cause no outside observations such as agreement or derision from a third party. It is simple and pure.

We were advised to think of any question to which we would like an answer, then to write it down. This done – listen to what comes first into your mind, and write that down. This is your answer – but you may not understand it – so you ask for clarification. Another question – listen again and write down what you 'hear'. Carry on in this way until you have the information you require. You will be surprised at the depth of understanding within your answer.

When this part of the Course was introduced to us I seemed to be at a crossroads along my intended pathway, but my question was simple – 'Where do I go from here?' I include my answers as an example of this kind of exercise.

Q. Where do I go from here?
A. You will work towards a greater understanding of all that is to be in the future.
Q. What will this involve?
A. You will find yourself involved in many things which will be new to you.
Q. Shall I meet new people this year?
A. Yes, as you travel your intended pathway you will find you come into contact with others who are at that point in your journey specifically in order to meet you.
Q. What for?
A. To discuss the information which we have given to you already. Some of which is in your unconscious mind.

Q. And will meeting these new people help to make that unconscious knowledge more readily available to me?
A. Yes. These new friends will also have acquired information in the same way and by discussing your thoughts and understanding at the level you have reached on that day, you will learn more from each other as you travel and talk together.
Q. Will these be people who have had UFO encounters too?
A. Mostly yes. Their extra-terrestrial memories have also been awakened, but there are others too who will be adding to your knowledge. It is an exciting pathway you are on now.

I found this exercise very helpful as it gave me an insight into the future and the part I would be playing in it – also it was confirmation that I was still on the right track.

Then later, after a meeting during which I wondered about any possible connection the subject matter could possibly have with UFOs. I was able to use this exercise again – and the answers I received were not at all what I expected.

CO-INCIDENCE – OR – WAS IT MEANT?

In 1975 I was given a one-year secondment by Northamptonshire Education Committee to pursue a course in The Teaching of Reading, leading to a Diploma in Educational Studies at the University of Leicester.

For a number of years I had been teaching Infants and when John Downing (in 1961) had introduced the Initial Teaching Alphabet (i.t.a) as an aid in the initial stages of teaching children to read the complexities of the spelling of the English language, I was encouraged by my Head Teacher to introduce it into my classroom.

So it was a natural progression for my Diploma to make a comparison between that and other phonetic alphabets which had been submitted for study at that time from people living in other countries worldwide, to enable students from those countries to more easily learn to read English as a second language.

I had found it to be a fascinating study so you can imagine my surprise when I attended a UFO meeting over 20 years later and found that one of the speakers was discussing an alphabet of a similar type.

She wrote our English alphabet (A-Z) on a blackboard, then above each letter she put a symbol. This was something I really understood. I was engrossed. As she wrote each new symbol above the corresponding alphabetical letter my logical mind tried to associate the alternative shapes with each familiar letter, so that if I needed to know and recognise them in the future I would be able to relate each new shape to the one I already knew.

As each English letter was given a different representation on the blackboard I was fascinated. There was silence in the room. At that moment all those years later I sat entranced, watching what could have been a progression to all the work I had done myself in the past.

The alphabetical symbols were completed on the blackboard and my analytical mind went into full gear. There was still silence in the room. I learned later that no one could understand the relevance of that exercise to UFOs – nor, if I am truthful, could I.

But there are 26 letters in the written English alphabet and there were only 24 in the corresponding one on the blackboard. That made sense to me because of my interest in the subject. Q is useless on its own. It always has to be followed by another letter, usually U as in QUICK, or now-a-days it can be followed by W as in QWERTY, but whichever additional letter is used the spoken sound is the same as it would be if 2 already used letters were combined e.g. KW. The same analysis applies to X. The spoken sound for X is KS as in FOX, so again 2 already used letters make the X as redundant as the Q, hence only 24 symbols are necessary instead of 26.

To me that had been an afternoon which brought back many happy memories of teaching children to read and of additional study during my teaching career.

Why this had been explained was not discussed but I knew that here was an example of truth about the spelling of our spoken language and I was left wondering whether in that way I was being shown that, although I have retired from that career I shall get even more pleasure from spreading the truth about something even more inexplicable viz. UFOs, and so be helping to increase an awareness of Spirit in others as I go into the future.

The memory of that afternoon stayed with me, but as I seemed to have been the only one at that meeting who could relate to any part of it I never found an answer that satisfied me, nor did I remember those new symbols.

I had asked questions of the speaker at the time, but when it became obvious that I knew more about phonetic alphabets than she did I felt it would be more tactful not to pursue the matter. So I accepted the fact that if I was meant to know then one day I would find out.

Then came the course which not only involved written and spoken communication with Spirit but also 'thought' communication, so I decided to see if I could find any answers in that way – and this is what happened.

THE ALPHABET

Q. I was fascinated by the content of this talk but can you tell me what relevance there is to it for us, please?

A. It is a Universal Alphabet which would be used phonetically for all to understand. Your own study of phonetic alphabets enabled you to understand what you were hearing and because of your studies it would not be foreign to you in any way.

Q. Would the other people in the room have understood its implications.

A. Not necessarily. It was an exercise to give the young lady added confidence in getting something across to a sceptical audience.
Q. Was my study on the Course I attended and the use of i.t.a. in schools a preparation for that afternoon?
A. Yes. All that you have learnt at any level has been a preparation for what is to come in the future.
Q. Can I include this episode in my next book as a co-incidence – being a specific and unlikely (unexpected) subject for discussion in connection with the subject of UFOs.
A. Yes. You realise that these topics can crop up when you least expect them.
Q. Are some of the topics raised at our meetings aimed especially at me?
A. Yes. Our messages to you are conveyed in them.
Q. Is it possible that I could be given the same information directly from you in my sleep, or in my writings?
A. Yes. We do that.
Q. Sometimes I feel pressured by people I meet. It is as if in some way they are wanting to control me, to have me running round in circles at their beck-and-call. Is it wrong to want to be my own person and do things my way?
A. No. You are right to think in that way. Be independent. Your confidence will grow. Your independence is important to you but do treat those others with respect. They are doing our work too, as you are all in your own individual ways and each is necessary for a satisfactory outcome.

This type of exercise can be used at any time especially when you need a deeper understanding of any point being raised.

ASTRAL TRAVEL

As yet I have no conscious recollection of having the ability to travel in this way, but the following incident gave me much food for thought regarding this subject.

I was attending a UFO conference when an announcement asked those present to please sit in the seat allocated to them when proceedings started again. Before this I had been involved in TV and Radio interviews and had missed the lectures during that time.

My admission ticket to the Conference (C20) meant that I had to ask six people to move so that I could sit in the seat allocated, right at the edge of the row and next to the wall.

As I passed, each one stood up and 'breathed in' until one lady remained seated and just moved her legs to one side, then the rest followed.

I particularly noticed this lady, not because she didn't stand up, but because whilst the others had given me a welcoming smile as I thanked them, this lady had a strange expression on her face. It was one which I couldn't explain. But I soon forget as I sat down and talked to the person who was seated next to me.

The lecture started and I became engrossed in its content. The next break arrived and we all filed out for refreshment – then returned. When I had nearly reached my seat there was a surprise in store for me.

The first lady spoke.

"About 12 to 15 years ago," she said, "I woke in the night and you were sitting at the bottom of my bed. I asked you why you were there, but you just smiled – and then you were gone."

I listened in amazement.

"I've told many people this story since that day," she continued, "and have carried her face in my memory. I have always wondered who she was, and as you came to sit down today I realised it was you."

"Do you travel at night?" she asked.

"Not that I know of," I replied, "but I do know that I am taught in my sleep, so perhaps I go on journeys as well without realising it."

That lady was convinced that I do and that I had visited her in that way.

SPREADING THE KNOWLEDGE

‘Go out into the world and spread the news
to help others to understand
that life continues into other worlds.
We are just passing through today,
stopping and learning as we do so.

Be grateful and gracious
and scatter what you gather to all ends of the earth,
for all to know.’

MY WORK

'You will be expected to speak out at meetings and conferences, telling audiences what it is that you are now receiving in your writings. You are finding now that you are having back-up material coming to you, which is reinforcing the information you received from other witnesses.

We like your way of explaining some points we would like you to raise, such as 'Spring-cleaning a corner of the Universe.' (*See below.)

This will help those less spiritually aware to understand. Your simple methods will work well.

Take the drawings with you and talk about them. There will be great interest in them, also in the poems. The one about the healing (p. 64) will be appropriate and the fishing (Appendix 4) one will amuse everyone, both gardeners and anglers alike.

Tell your story simply, factually and truthfully. Keep to these points, but you have some amusing tales as well.

Speak about us with affection. Let everyone know that there is nothing to fear. We will be with you all and some people may see us. We will guide you along this new pathway – a journey which you are now beginning.'

*My analogy for this is –

Like the housewife who is proud of her home so God is proud of the home he created for us at the beginning of time.

Unfortunately mankind is proving to be a far from efficient 'housekeeper' and as our planet becomes more and more unbalanced, so it will in time become less and less suitable for human habitation.

It is obvious now that repairs are becoming necessary, and like us, when we spring-clean our rooms the contents are moved out to enable the work to be done more quickly.

Work is going on now in the background to make sure that our planet survives the growing devastation in our part of the Universe. To do this it has to be upgraded from the third dimension to the fifth.

A force of UFO Spaceships from other dimensions is waiting in space to 'spring-clean' our part of the Universe and to update our planet, to rebalance, refresh, recharge and revive it.

Whilst this is happening we shall be taken safely to the Spaceship which is the correct one for us at our level of Spiritual awareness.

Then, after the Earth's energy has been renewed we shall all return to re-inhabit the earth, which by then will have been transformed to a higher dimensional level.

TALKS

Over the last few years I have done what I would class as a series of talks about my UFO experience and my life after it, using the information recorded in my first book ONE STEP BEYOND plus anything else which has happened up to the date of the meeting.

At each I have drawn from the same fund of material, information which I have gathered for 20 years in a variety of forms e.g. UFO encounter, mediumship, writings, artwork, poems, etc., but each talk turned out to be different in some way.

Points I have felt it necessary to emphasise on one occasion have been totally ignored on another. Some are more UFO orientated, some are more Spiritually orientated. I go to each with the same general knowledge of my subject but in each there has seemed later to have been a different point of emphasis.

I noticed too that when I stopped in 'mid-flight' to make a conscious effort to decide in which direction to go next, that decision seemed to be made for me, as I would 'see' a picture or 'hear' a word at that time which would lead me towards another point to be raised. Then afterwards when I assessed the talks, each seemed to be so effortless and it became obvious to me that I was, at that time, definitely in receipt of Spiritual Guidance.

A message I received at that time reads:–

'The tides of time are passing quickly. You are doing your talks and meeting people new to you, some with a deep interest in what you have to say, others who are more interested in everyday activities. But they heard part of your news and will be thinking about your words.

Do not be despondent if those at meetings seem to be disinterested. They made the effort to turn up, so some seeds of thought have been sown and we will add to these as time goes by.

Your talks have been a series, each of which has been similar, yet very different. There has always been someone especially there to receive your messages. There have also always been some there who cannot understand. That has been a test for you.'

I had already become aware that certain people present were more interested than others. They asked interesting questions and stayed behind to find out more. Equally it was obvious there were some who came into the other category as the following examples will show.

Before the night of one meeting I wondered why I had been asked at all to speak to this particular group. The Chairman for that evening thought the expected audience would cope with the UFO experience but it was made very clear to me that under no circumstances was I to mention Spiritualism or Healing. I was far from pleased about this as I had been invited purely because that Chairman had himself followed my progress over the years and had been fascinated by each new experience. It was as if he felt the listeners needed protection from something and that I did not understand.

I gave it a great deal of thought and discussed it with friends.

'It's your story,' they said, 'and that's what he asked you to talk about. How can you possibly pick out bits of it to suit an audience you have never met? Anyway – Spirit will guide you.'

So when the appropriate time arrived I started in my usual way. The audience seemed absorbed. I had suggested beforehand that they should interrupt if someone did not understand what I said – but no one did. One lady smiled at me each time I looked in her direction, some of the men looked very thoughtful, but no one was fidgety. I had completely forgotten the chairman and I was in full flow.

I mentioned my visit to Charles Chapman, the Medium and Healer from Rugby and naturally followed with my own development as a Spiritual Healer, then on to my writings and I passed around my Psychic Artwork which aroused much interest. I was absorbed in it all.

Then a voice to my side said, 'Five minutes,' and brought me back to reality. I rounded off my talk and sat down. I felt happy with what I had said and I had completely forgotten the restrictions I had been given before the meeting.

A lady to the left of me glared at the Organiser of the group. 'I don't know how you could possibly invite a woman like her to speak to a group like this,' she said, 'this is a Church group and she's a Spiritualist, and the Bible says . . .' and she quoted many passages from it. When she stopped talking I was asked if I would like to respond.

'As a Church person,' I heard myself saying, 'your top man is God. I am Church of England and my top man is God, and when I do the healing I am a channel for that Healing energy which passes through me to the patient. That comes from a Supreme Being whom I also know as GOD. So I think that you and I actually have a great deal in common.'

But she was not impressed. 'This is the first of these meetings I have ever come to,' she said, 'and I shall never come again,' and out she walked. No one seemed to know who she was or where she had come from, but I was told before I left for home that my talk had engendered a great deal of discussion during refreshment time and that had never happened before. They were pleased about that.

However the one thing about that evening which stands out most prominently in my memory was when a man came to speak to me afterwards. He had been pointed out to me when I arrived as someone who suffered from epilepsy as he had unfortunately had a fit during a previous meeting.

He asked me if I could put him in touch with a Healing Group in the area in which he lived. This I was able to do and in response he punched the air with his fist and yelled out, 'YIPPEE! HOPE after 32 years.'

Ignoring the Chairman's restrictions on the content of my talk had obviously been the right thing to do.

Another of my talks was held in a Community Centre where, quite near to the lecture room was a bar containing a television set. It was a strange experience as I talked to see members of the audience disappearing at intervals, then returning with full glasses of drink.

But the most surprising thing happened during the interval when one of the organisers said to the other (who was standing by my side) 'Will you total up the money when she starts to speak again? I'm going to watch the football match.'

Most talks are done in town venues but occasionally I am invited to do one in someone's home, or in a village hall. These are very friendly and most informal evenings, small groups of interested people in an informal atmosphere who ask some very searching questions.

Spirit is right when I am told that there will be someone at every meeting who has come especially to hear what I have to say; those who stay behind afterwards to discuss a point, or those interested in my artwork such as art teachers, including one who wanted an opinion on her own work. This of course is something which I can't do because they are artists in their own right. I am not. My art work is Spiritually inspired and controlled. It needs no conscious thought on my part and no preparation. The pen in my hand is controlled by an external influence and the final result has a much deeper meaning than I could ever foresee. And there was the fellow abductee who couldn't resist saying, 'I told you 3 years ago that you'd be talking like this, didn't I? But you said you couldn't see that happening, didn't you? But here you are doing just that.'

Touché – point proven!

WORKING WITH SPIRIT

MY ROLE

'We will now talk about the way we shall work together and about the messages we shall give you to pass on when the opportunity arises.

We shall call on you as we do now. We shall plant thoughts in your mind which you will be able to transfer to paper as you are doing now, or you will hear our voice more clearly and definite words will be relayed to you clairaudiently. This will happen when it is important to relay some information we give to someone you are, at that time, in contact with. You have seen other Mediums do it and you will become proficient at this too.

We will not put you in a position of embarrassment. You will always be able to manage the situation confidently. So do not worry. It will be a new experience for you and we have often noticed that you do enjoy these.

The earth-friends you have now will understand your messages from us and will support and encourage you. Those who don't, will in time become more Spiritually aware and will then be able to do so.

You have the patience and understanding to do this work well.'

Then later –

'Your journey on this pathway has started and much will be accomplished. Your work will be enjoyable and rewarding spiritually. You will meet many new people who will be expecting the news you offer. Your field of vision and understanding will widen as new perceptions flow into your heart.

You will be blessed with the wisdom to guide others. You will appear to calm them. This will be an inner calmness which will become apparent – a kind of magnetism will draw people to you. They will listen and know that what you are saying is the truth.

Of course there will be some who do not understand, but they too will listen – then think about what they have heard. This will be the beginning of their transformation.

THE CONSIDERATION GIVEN TO WHAT IS HEARD IS THE BEGINNING OF AN ANALYSIS OF THE SPOKEN WORD, LEADING TO A BETTER UNDERSTANDING OF IT.'

STRENGTH

'You will need to be strong. You will find you have trials to overcome along your pathway. You must not be complacent. You must continue to be positive in everything you do. We shall always be with you to guide you along the way.

You are preparing yourself for any obstacles which may occur during your talks. There will be those who try to trip you up, but you will remain steadfast to the end. Your calmness will manifest itself.

Bridges will be built and crossed. You will know what we mean on the day. Some you have not met before will surprise you with understanding. You are all receiving our messages now. Spread these far and wide and as the great day comes nearer trumpets will be sounded for all to hear.

The Great Man cometh. All will be well with the World. Be strong. Go forward and honour your God.'

MISSIONS

'Information will be coming to you and those of you with missions will be guided into them in a very natural way so as not to cause much disruption in your lives.

You have your mission Elsie. It is to spread the truth about us in your naturally simplistic way so that all will be understood.

We are giving you information which you will need so that you will be ready and will have it to hand when the opportunity arises.'

'The light shines from you leading the way for others to follow. You are doing our work well. Your interest in each new detail is obvious and you are going out of your way to add to the knowledge we are giving you. As you search so others gain knowledge too.

Your way is smooth and long and even. You have been tested recently and have known to ask for our help when the negative side of things has built up. We are here to help you, you know that.'

TRAINING

'We have been training you for some time now in your sleep state, giving you information which you will need in the future. As you need it so it will become available to you and you will use it competently and with a very confident manner.

You will enjoy this new commitment in your 'retirement'. Retirement for you will not be dull. It will entail talks, travelling, and a lot of media contact.'

Following a Conference in Staffordshire where I felt it had become necessary to emphasise the Spiritual side of my work I received the following –

WHAT ARE CONFERENCES FOR?

'There were many people at the Conference who were ready to hear your news and were awakened by what they heard.

Conferences should be held to open people's minds. Many were there to hear controversial information. What is given at these functions should be food for thought, giving the recipient that which he/she needs to add to that which has already been accepted, to develop further the understanding which will be required in the future when all will be revealed.

Much new information came to you all yesterday. Much more is yet to come and it will arrive in many different ways, some at expected times and some when least expected. But it will develop as and when you are each ready to accept it. Go ahead as you are doing now. Your pathway is smooth, forward, and along level ground. Your goal is in sight.'

HELPING EACH OTHER

'To help each other is very important at all times, not just at Christmas time which you class as the season of goodwill. Goodwill should be spread at all times. We should all be conscious of those less able than ourselves.

There is always some-one we can help no matter how incompetent we may feel. We all have a skill, or a piece of knowledge which will help the next man to further an understanding of some point raised. At every educational level you will find someone at a lower level who will benefit from something you have just learned.

And from that contact you will witness the pleasure from that added sense of achievement which you have then passed on, and from within you will glow with a pleasure which expresses a satisfaction which warms your heart. You have passed on a gift and you have a new friend.

WORDS OF WISDOM COST NOTHING BUT KINDNESS AND IN RETURN YOU HAVE RECEIVED LOVE AND GRATITUDE.'

INTO THE FUTURE

'Your heart will be gladdened and all that is good will come your way as you accomplish what you were born to do. As it all unfolds there will be a lightness in your heart and you will find that all you need to convey to others will flow, seemingly with no effort at all.

Your circle of contact will increase and more will ask for Healing help from you, and although it all takes time it will be as if the time stretches, yet there is time to relax too.

You will go about things with love in your heart for your fellow beings and love given is always returned.

Go ahead. Spread our words to all who will listen. As you go around so you will meet them, and you will be surprised who they are. Some will be those you least expect, so giving you many unexpected surprises. A joyful time, one of harmony with one and all. One of courage to carry the word into a wilderness of disbelievers and sceptics.

But your ways of delivering our message, both simply and truthfully will prove to be the best method and prove to be peaceful in the end.

Joy be with you.'

Further messages from Spirit summed up the situation, offering sound advice and explaining the reasons for it – and if heeded by us all would save us and our planet a great deal of distress.

WORKING TOGETHER

'The ways of the worldly life are beyond comprehension at times. So many cause so much trouble for others. Life would be so much happier if everyone pulled together and worked cohesively for the good of mankind and the world itself.

Love towards each other would rid the people of so much disharmony and unpleasantness. A smile and a cheery word cost nothing and multiply one hundred fold as they are passed on one to another.

A SMILE

Give a smile this very day
To everyone around
It will be returned to you
And Friendships will abound.

A smile can brighten the dullest day
And make the recipient glad.
You've made a friend along the way
You never knew you had.

A smile that it exchanged
Can make a friendship grow,
Bringing to the both of you
More pleasure than you know.

Also to many others
As it's continually passed along
From him to her, from them to us,
Encompassing everyone.

The simple smile that first you gave
Has now touched many hearts,
Showing how successfully
A loving friendship starts.

GOOD ADVICE

'Do not go anywhere with anger in your heart. Listen to all sides of the question which are put forward and balance each in your heart to reach a positive conclusion.

Never act on a negative thought. That negative thought becomes a negative action and spreads distrust causing sadness.

Wait and hear what is spoken before deciding how to reply. There will be much less stress then to cope with and you could be surprised at how much time this supposition of future events can take; time which can be better spent on the positive and loving actions which are always there waiting to be put into operation.

Spread love around. Use your time wisely. Your energy will be renewed as you do so. Also others will benefit too.

This is good advice to you all.'

THE WEATHER

'The winds of change are blowing now and you will observe many things which will be new to you, but it will be as if you have always understood.

There will be no need to be afraid. We shall be with you and your family – and you will be safe.

A new world is coming. You must be prepared. You will be prepared. You will be ready and will know, when that time comes, exactly what your role will be – and you will do it with understanding and without questioning it.'

The heart of England, the centre it be,
Is the middle of land far away from the sea

Where you will be safe when winter storms blow
And cause massive waves on the seashores to grow.

Not only the beach but also the land
Will be battered by these, nothing can withstand.

You don't expect the sea to flow on the land
But happen it will, when all that is planned

Gives way under pressure, erodes all in its path
And changes the coastline under the sea's wrath.

The strong winds will come battering us all
And in their wake barriers will fall.

The elements have strength to counteract all
Even the strength of a man-built sea-wall.

Dear God. Keep us safe when this hazard arrives.
Allow us to live. Please save our lives.

Give each of us strength to be able to see
That most important of all is loyalty to Thee.

Amen.

This poem was given to me on 4th November 1996 and I was reminded of it in January 1998 when a red alert was declared along the Sussex Coast because of severe weather conditions. Members of our family living there were on the receiving end of 100 mph winds. A tornado hit a town a few miles from where they lived and a sea wall was breached.

Then again in April 1998 when over much of the country, continuous rain caused many rivers to overflow and the most serious flooding was experienced for about 150 years. In my own part of the country where the rivers Nene and Ouse flow there were floods 3 to 4 feet deep in Weedon, Northampton and the surrounding areas.

'The wind is rough again. More storm damage could be done. March winds and April showers at this time of the year you will automatically assume. But the weather patterns have changed considerably since your childhood.

Some fields are still under water since the lengthy spells of rain a few months ago, the ground unable to soak any more of it away.

Your earth has had another mild winter and as gardeners will observe there have been few frosts to kill the garden pests. The flies have wintered well in cracks and window frames as you have noticed. Never before have you seen so many.

The weather is changing and not for the better. More unpleasant conditions are yet to come, stronger winds, heavy rainfall, a very hot summer – all unsettling the stratas of the earth and making volcanic eruptions much more likely – and sadly an almost certain loss of life.'

'The wind is rough on your planet and only man is to blame. The ice-caps are melting. The earth is tilting on its axis. The seasons as you knew them in your childhood have ceased to exist.

The bridges will collapse with the greater flow of water under them. Farming land is being continually flooded. Animals, plants and people all suffer. The devastation of the earth continues. It must be stopped if humanity is not to suffer.

Spread the word. Governments must act.'

'The sticks will soon be crackling as they burn in the open fireplaces, bringing warmth and comfort to those sitting near.

Outside the icy winds will blow from the north bringing snow everywhere. On the better days the sun will shine through, bringing hope of new life and new expectations to all.

Be prepared for the thunder and lightning flashes warning not to become too complacent. The weather patterns are quite temperamental and sometimes give no warning of a sudden change.

Do all you can to be able to cope with the unexpected. Spread love everywhere and raise the balance of a heightened awareness around you and all will be well for you.

We will be with you. We will guide you towards a much smoother pathway where the waters flow calmly and you will be safe. Spread the word.'

'Tonight the wind blows strongly and the seas batter the shores. The snow you have seen is a sample of what is to come. Sudden and unexpected changes in the weather patterns causing problems and inconveniences to all.

Your hearth will be filled,
Your fire will burn bright
And all will be well
For you and yours tonight.

Be aware of all this for you will need to know as changes come. We shall be working on your planet to make life on it more pleasurable. The dead wood will be removed and that which is left will burn more brightly. A new awareness will be coming to all to brighten the days ahead.

Remain strong and all will be well. You have nothing to fear.'

CONSEQUENCES

'The birds in the trees bring their joyous songs to you. At this time of your year many are spreading their wings to fly to warmer climates. Sadly many will not reach their destinations. Lakes will have dried up and vegetation will have been destroyed. The usual vegetation where they rest on their way will have disappeared this year as the earth continues to disintegrate. The thoughtlessness of humankind for his fellow beings is the cause. Even weather changes can be classed as man-made.

So much is taken for granted now. Planning for a future seems to be a thing of the past. Hope seems to be fading and effort does not appear worthwhile in such a negative atmosphere.

Attitudes must change if all is to be saved – and it is not a matter of money. Love is given freely, a commodity which can only cause pleasure. This will cause smiles all round, given and received. A new positive outcome so easy to achieve is all that is required. Encourage this always. You will be surprised how much better life will seem. A new feeling of upliftment will be felt by everyone whose heart is receptive and a new purpose in life will be found.

All the damage done can be reversed with continued positive thought and working towards a future of love and understanding towards a new awareness of Spiritual Love.

Continue on your way along this road of achievement to a very bright future.'

'The Commemorative Day Celebrations gave the older people the opportunity to remember – but also to make comparisons if they so wished. Comparisons regarding the state of life today with that of 50 years ago, not only in the state of the Nations but in the state of living conditions.

The housing situation is better, but the conditions regarding the atmosphere have deteriorated. Different types of illness abound, many caused by these changes.

The sun shines. The day is warmer. People suffer from Asthmatic attacks. Some die. The ozone layer has been penetrated. Harmful rays of sunlight can penetrate it – all to man's detriment. All caused by man's incompetence and thoughtlessness.

In this way the thoughtlessness of a few affects the health of many. Those incapable of helping themselves suffer greatly. Some, for greater financial benefit, have little consideration for others.

SELFISHNESS and GREED abound on the earth for all to see. It is a sad time for humanity. The earth needs help. It is coming to you.'

'The tomb of Tutankhamen has revealed many of the mysteries of the East because of disturbances caused by man. His actions elsewhere in the world are causing an imbalance of the planet earth. Man should change his behaviour and work towards a more Spiritual understanding. The devastation of the earth planet can only cause it to deteriorate and become uninhabitable.

This small happening in our large universe will result in an imbalance in the cosmos and will affect us all.'

DAMAGE LIMITATION

'The wickedness in the world increases and unless mankind changes his ways will overcome the good needed to achieve all things.

Spread love and happiness around. Keep cheerful and balanced in all things. Give love to everyone you meet and all will be well.

So much love and Healing are needed now to improve the state of the life led by most. Give willingly and rewards will flow.

Kindness costs nothing and reaps one hundred-fold. The love you spread will be returned in many different ways to benefit all.'

'We in Spirit are watching over you, guiding and guarding you. We have your well-being at heart and will lead you towards the light, showing you the way forward for all to follow.

Go ahead with love in your hearts for your fellow men and love will spread to all.

Be kind, unselfish, uncritical and positive in your actions. Encourage others to do the same and this new awareness will have a Healing effect on a very damaged planet.

All unselfish acts can spread goodness and love and repair much of the damage already done. Go forward in this way and do good to your fellow beings.'

EVACUATION

'This picture depicts three satellite ships awaiting the evacuation exercise. We are ready as your Earth is gradually becoming uninhabitable.'

'Out in space our ships are waiting as you know. Look and you will see our signals. We are ready, in case disaster prevails, to keep humanity safe from harm.

Simple daily acts by man can multiply and cause a grand scale of devastation. Once started it cannot be stopped if the stupidity continues, even by only a few.

Everyone must work together for the good of a project. One dissenter can cause the failure of all. You must all be as one. Work together and create with love a new positive attitude towards all living things.

Your efforts will be rewarded in the end. Your good doings will be magnified and the new earth will be ready for Our Saviour's return. Start now.'

'The movement across the vast areas of space is something spectacular to behold, but none can match those which certain people are privileged to see – what your people call UFOs.

These craft come from other dimensions in space and can travel vast distances in a remarkably short space of time. Nothing on your earth can match them.

Ashtar and his command wait in an area outside the Earth's dimension to withdraw those whose requirements meet those necessary for future evacuation. The ships are ready. Many are waiting like you to be called.

The programme to raise the awareness of Spirit by the spreading of Love and Light is not progressing fast enough. More needs to be done more quickly.

Do your bit and let others recognise the calmness and tranquillity which you exude. Others will then follow. This is a Damage-Limitation Programme and all will not then be lost.

Do your best.'

'Noah's Ark was built to save the animals of the earth and Noah's family, at the time of the great flood.

When it becomes necessary to evacuate life forms from the Earth again it will be done by spaceships from other dimensions in the universe.

Those who have aspired to a greater Spiritual awareness during their lifetimes will be transported off their planet whilst it is upgraded and purified. When all this, and more is done it will again be suitable for habitation and you will all be returned.

You have no need to worry. Everything will go smoothly. There will be no panic. All will be well and you will all be safe. Have no fear.'

'The evacuation of the Earth will be accomplished satisfactorily. You all have a place where you will grow in Spiritual awareness and come face to face with the Master.'

'AS BIG AS A FOOTBALL PITCH'

Since becoming a Healer I have felt very strongly that my UFO experience was a Spiritual one as there was no fear involved only fascination.

This theory had been impossible for some UFO researchers to take on board and I began to meet the same reaction from them as I had from sceptics in 1978 when the encounter had taken place. Then over a period of years a series of occurrences seemed to prove to me the validity of this conclusion and I believe that I finally have an assurance that will illustrate that it really was a Spiritual encounter.

At one UFO meeting I attended in 1992 a gentleman present said that he had a message for everyone in the room and stated that we can all expect an enormous shock in the future when a massive explosion will occur on the earth planet, but we in the room (and our families) need not fear this because UFO spaceships as big as football pitches would come down and take us off, there to live until the earth settles down again when we shall all be returned to continue our lives here.

In the notes I had taken at that meeting I had written that this man was dressed entirely in black and that I felt he talked as if he were programmed.

He also said that one-quarter of the earth's population were three-quarters alien and later singled me out to assure me that I HAD been in a UFO during my missing time where I had been given information which, when the time is right I shall pass on to others in my destined role as a teacher. He finished by saying that an important man would come to earth but gave no further information on that subject.

By this time we were all spell-bound by these unexpected claims which seemed quite unconnected with the topic discussed by the main speaker that afternoon. We had been taken completely by surprise and those who were not UFO witnesses had difficulty in understanding the relevance of its inclusion – and many people present made it very clear that they came into that category.

I decided that the best plan where I was concerned was to tell no one about this until I received some kind of confirmation.

Whoever would believe there could be UFOs 'as big as football pitches'? It was this description of the UFOs which intrigued me the most and at that time the fear of ridicule still haunted me. So I decided that to wait and see what materialised (if indeed anything did) would be the safest bet, although I was equally worried about disappearing suddenly off the face of the earth with no opportunity to say, 'Goodbye'.

Later I realised that this could have happened to me before during my 'missing time' (22nd November 1978) and if so I had returned then, so perhaps it would be an experience such as that. At that time there had been a continuation of my life before the experience with seemingly no interruption at all, so I assume that the same thing would be the case if it became necessary in the future.

Then I became part of a Healing Group and exactly a year after that meeting an elderly lady arrived for some Healing.

'Do tell Elsie about your dream,' I heard a voice suggest.

'She won't be interested,' was the response.

'Try me,' I asked – and this is what I heard.

She'd had a dream about an air crash. It had been during daylight and she had been standing in the field behind her home. As she looked up, high in the sky she could see a dark object the shape of a 'Goodyear' balloon but squarer at the front and back. Its only movement seemed to be downwards as it was getting larger as she watched it.

On the underside there appeared to be a darker recess which she described as being like a hovercraft without its skirts. Suddenly it got very much bigger and she realised that it was out of control. It was swooping from side to side, but there was no noise.

In the final stages it descended so rapidly that it must have been falling at hundreds of feet per second and as it hit the ground it raised a cloud of dust and earth.

The corner nearest to her had been the first to hit the ground and it had given a double bounce before finally settling in the field next to the one in which she stood, so she could then assess its size which she estimated was 'as big as a football pitch'. She could also then see port-hole like windows on two levels around the craft.

Her next thought had been for the people on board and the number 500 sprang into her mind. She thought she was the only witness to this so she phoned the Rescue Services.

Soon she became aware that the Police had cordoned off the road and that ambulances had arrived. She could hear screams and shouts coming from inside the wrecked craft but there was no fire or smoke. She concluded by saying that the craft appeared to be built of the same magnetic material as the USA's Stealth Bombers.

This was a very vivid account which recorded so many precise details. We all listened in silence, but in my mind I was reminded of the facts which had been forecast at our meeting exactly twelve months before.

I have always felt that my UFO encounter was a Spiritual one. Healing is a

Spiritual experience too. The lady who gave that amazing account had come to me for Healing. If I had not become a Healer there would have been no reason at all for us ever to have met.

This had been described as a dream, but during the next two weeks two more people from another village in the area also reported to me having seen a UFO at approximately the same time. So many details in their accounts were identical, even to the description of the size of the craft – 'as big as a football pitch' – their actual words too.

In just over a year I had heard that expression four times, but the surprises did not stop there.

One of the things I enjoy most in connection with UFOs is to attend a Conference. There I meet many people on my wavelength and I can never remember ridicule being aimed at me on any of those occasions during the last 20 years. Everyone is there because of a genuine interest in the subject and the reaction I usually receive is one of envy because it is a subject I can speak about with complete confidence because of personal experience. So it came as no real surprise that it was at such a venue that I received information to add to this.

How it came about was really the most unexpected part of all. When booking to attend the event I had added extra to the admission fees to cover the cost of a single room at the Hotel. Unfortunately these bookings had been underestimated and those of us hoping for a single room were asked if we minded sharing with another visitor.

Eventually it was all sorted out and I found myself sharing a room with a lady UFO Investigator who had so many interesting tales to tell that we talked until the early hours of the next morning – and the one thing that remains in my memory from that night was that she had been called out many times to see and then write reports on UFOs which were 'as big as three football pitches'.

This was the first time I had ever imagined a UFO as large as that but it did help to understand accounts I read later from other parts of the world where even larger UFOs were seen supposedly then waiting to take what was described as 'the fallen ones' off this planet.

Because of this series of events I have been made aware that when the state of the earth becomes uninhabitable due to man's inconsiderate behaviour, those who are taken to safety in very large-sized UFOs will find enough room to be comfortable on the journey, then later, when the Earth has been cleansed, upgraded and realigned to a higher dimension within the Universe we will be returned to live again in peace and love – perhaps then with the important man mentioned at that first meeting.

This could be the return of Christ, the man I heard about in my Sunday School class (p. 25) and if so then the promise I made to myself all those years ago will have been fulfilled.

A NEW WORLD

'The most you can expect from any other being is exactly what you would be prepared to give yourself in a similar circumstance.

If you can give love, so you will be given love in return. If you smile at someone you will know that that will be returned also. These are two things which cost nothing but which give much pleasure to the recipient.'

YOUR ROLE AS A HUMAN SPIRIT

'Our messages to you continue and you now understand more about your role as a Human Spirit.

As you know you chose to be who you are in order to awaken other extra-terrestrials' minds to a greater understanding of what is to come.

Continue on that road. Spread love and positive thought so that other minds will awaken to that which you all know because of your encounters in the past.

This world is awakening now and you will be playing your part. Those you alert to this will awaken others and love will spread and the earth will be saved.

Continue as you have started, the way is along level ground. You will speak; you will be heard; and you will be understood. We will be by your side.'

I NOW KNOW

I NOW KNOW the purpose was
To awaken the memory
Of a previous life out there in space
For a purpose we've yet to see.

That we are being trained
For that we were born to do,
To change the attitude of man
This planet to renew.

And bring a positive feeling
To all that does occur,
Spreading TRUTH & LOVE everywhere –
A pleasure to be sure.

TOWARDS A NEW BEGINNING

'Conferences should be held to open people's minds. What is given at these functions should be food for thought, giving the recipient understanding which will be required in the future when all will be revealed.'

This had been given to me earlier by Spirit and I was reminded of it at the Northampton UFO Research Group's Annual Seminar on 8th August 1998 when one of the topics suggested for discussion was 'UFOs are messengers of a forthcoming catastrophe'. Some thought that 'devastation' would have been a more appropriate description, but whichever wording was used it was so negative that it could only result in despair.

The 22nd November was the 20th anniversary of the strangest and most unexpected happening I could possibly have foreseen. I had entered the World of Ufology in a state of complete ignorance and with a gigantic hope that I would find a complete answer to it all if I asked enough questions.

I needed to know – What was it that I drove under on that day? Where had it come from? Why was it there? Why did no one else admit to seeing it although there were many others driving under it too? Could it have been there especially for me and if so why? A catalogue of questions but no answers were forthcoming.

Although during the years as I was writing ONE STEP BEYOND, I did find some of the answers, I was still expecting that others more involved both nationally and internationally would be able to supply me with the overall truth about the experience, but it never happened.

Many claims were made, which we who had experienced this strangeness found we could not accept, and gradually as time passed it became apparent that those who would eventually 'know' would be the Witnesses themselves, because information had been coming to each of us as an inner awareness at our own levels of understanding.

We found we were each being given a very special piece of information which, when the time is right will be made known to us. This will fit together with that which others have been given, so encompassing everyone worldwide and enabling us to go into the planned New World on a higher level of Spiritual awareness, a place where positive thoughts and love for one another are paramount – a world where hope abounds and negativity no longer prevails.

We all have an important part to play in this. Our mission has been defined and as new information continues to be added to that which we have already been given, so we shall be joined by others travelling along this same pathway. A very exciting future lies ahead for us all.

On the day of that Seminar the UFO witnesses present were able to redress the balance. We had all begun to notice that 'things' were happening, nothing which at the time you could really put your finger on and remark as being something particularly special, but which, when you looked back over a period of time had become a noticeable observation.

I was aware of this too. Over many months, maybe a year or so, much had happened in my life which had come about in such a way as to be almost imperceptible, yet each left its mark on my memory and later they combined to make me realise that in a very subtle way, so gradually and so sensitively there was this realisation of wonderment that it had all been building up towards a NEW BEGINNING.

It has been a process involving a total cleansing not only of the physical planet on which we live, but also within our minds in order to fit us for this new land which we shall inherit, where life will continue in a situation of Love, Truth and Peace which will then reign within us all for ever.

'LET THE LIGHT SHINE FROM YOUR SOULS so that everyone can see that all is well with you and that the love of God is within you, encompassing you and enfolding you.

Go on your journey safely and offer the HAND OF FRIENDSHIP to all you meet. All will be well.'

Jellicoe and Joseph.

APPENDIX 1

On the 22nd November 1978 at about 1.30 pm when a colleague and I were preparing to leave a Chinese Restaurant in Daventry I felt a tightening sensation around my head and thought I was going to faint. It was as if a band of material had been put across my forehead and around my head and was being pulled tighter and tighter.

Suddenly it stopped as surprisingly as it had started. The pain which lasted for only about a minute had disappeared completely.

After my day's duties at the Daventry Teachers' Centre were completed I phoned my husband to tell him I was leaving. I gathered together my belongings, locked the premises, then walked to the car and checked the lights. The left-hand front side-light was not functioning. It had been a lovely sunny day and wispy grey clouds were just appearing in the blue sky, so at 5.15 pm, driving on dipped headlights, I started my journey home along the A45 to Weedon.

At the traffic lights there I turned right on the A5 to travel towards Towcester.

Ahead of me I could see two very bright lights, one red and one green, immediately above the road along which I was to travel. My immediate thought was that this must be a very low-flying aircraft which would soon zoom over my head. But there were buildings on each side of the road between it and me and it seemed low enough to crash into them and then land on top of the car. There was a lot of traffic on the A5 at that time of day and strangely it seemed as if everything had gone into slow motion. A crash seemed inevitable but for some inexplicable reason I knew I would be safe.

Suddenly I realised that it was not moving at all. It seemed to be stationary and I travelled towards it with my nose practically pressed on the windscreen. I knew that in the time I had before I drove directly underneath it I would have to collect as much information as I could about it.

I looked hard at it. In the darkening sky I could see a form which I would describe as a dumb-bell shaped aerial object with a brilliant red light under the left sphere and an equally brilliant green light under the other. It was grey in colour, blending in well with the grey wispy clouds accumulating above it and it appeared to be made of a very smooth plastic-type material. This 'thing' was considerably wider than the road, and was estimated later to have been about fifty feet in length and a hundred to one hundred and fifty feet above it.

As I approached it I could see no windows or openings anywhere and I felt compelled to stop and find out more, but the A5 was (and still is) a very busy trunk road. I could hear nothing unusual at that particular time and drove immediately underneath it.

To reach my home in Church Stowe I had to turn off the A5 at the top of the hill in this section of the road and by then I was completely intrigued by the sighting of such an extraordinary craft. After turning, the hill continues and there I was able to stop and look back. Here it was safe to do so and I wanted to see whether it was still in the same position over the A5. I gave a sigh of relief. It was – and at that point I was about level with it, being rewarded with the other side view then as well as the one I'd had from underneath. I stood for a moment marvelling at its structure and noticing again the smoothness of the outline. What was this strange craft?

Then, as if to further attract my attention, the green light started to flash. Was it some kind of signal, I wondered, and if so what was it signifying and to whom was it being sent?

Church Stowe is a very small village high on a hill and travelling along the country road towards it I was able to look back and observe those two lights which remained in the same position. In that half mile or so of road I looked back three times and each time the green light was flashing but the red one was not.

About half a mile from the A5 I turned right into the village and it was here that I turned, in second gear, but when I changed up to third gear something most unusual happened. My foot was hard on the accelerator pedal which was then flat on the floor of the car. There was no sound from the engine at all. The car was slowing down and had almost reached the point of stopping.

The sensation of an accelerator pedal actually touching the floor of the car whilst it was moving was a new experience for me. I told myself not to panic but to start from scratch and see what happened. I did not switch on the engine (the red ignition lights were not on), I changed from third gear to first and depressed the accelerator. To my surprise and relief the car started normally and I was able to continue on my way.

I changed from first to second gear, then up to third gear again and I travelled happily along the next 100 metres or so of road. Here it was bordered on both sides by trees and the highest branches of these formed a canopy above the road, which gave the impression of travelling through a tunnel.

I remember reaching the end of the trees. Then the next thing I knew was that the car was stationary, the natural light had disappeared and everything was in absolute blackness. My engine had stopped. My lights were out. Everything was black, dark, velvety blackness. I knew I was sitting in the car, my hands were on the steering wheel but I could not see the car, the road, the buildings or the trees. I had no idea where I was at all. I wondered where all the lights had gone and how it could have happened so suddenly. I felt strangely calm and unafraid.

Then suddenly, at that very moment, a brilliant white circle of light about a metre in diameter shone on the road to the left of the car by the passenger door. It lit up the road and I could see that the car was stationary beside the farm gate about fifty yards further on from the tree-covered part of the road – and that I had travelled round a right-angled bend in that section of the road. The light went off and I sat in darkness again. Then another circle of light shone towards the left-hand front of the car and went out. Lights then continued to flash onto the ground, on and off, on and off, in a semi-circle around the front of the car from left to right, each punctuating the darkness and assuring me that I was still in the village and on my way home. This sequence was then repeated in a semi-circle in the opposite direction, from right to left back to where they started.

I was absolutely fascinated and sat watching as each one shone taking into my mind the completely circular shape of each light as it lit up the road, its whiteness and its brilliance. I could not recall ever having seen any light so pure, nor yet so circular in shape. Then they repeated the route from left to right again and I began to realise that I was counting them too. The last one shone in the garden of the cottage to my right. It was then as if it was turned. It shone upwards from the garden to the roof on the front of the building and was switched off.

After the last light had gone out the whole area was in complete darkness. I have never seen Church Stowe in such darkness. It was absolutely black. Again I could see neither the houses nor the road, not even the car I was sitting in. then as I sat in the darkness, astounded by this phenomenon, I calmly decided to analyse it all. I thought there had been fifteen light circles which had shone onto the road plus the one which shone on the garden. That one, for some reason, seemed to be more important than the others. I wondered why it had given me that impression? Was it showing me that there was something above the car at that point? But I had seen no beams with those lights to indicate this.

I was absolutely fascinated by all this and very curious. I looked upward through the car windscreen but saw only a blackness everywhere and expressing my surprise aloud, I said "Good Gracious". My car was stationary – but the very next moment, as if someone had pulled a switch, the enveloping darkness was replaced by natural daylight. I could again see the village and I was driving my car normally about thirty yards further along the road from the farm gate, in third gear as I had been when I reached the end of the trees. I changed down to second gear to negotiate the other right-angled bend in the village, this one by St Michael's Church, and I was conscious of a feeling of relief as I drove round it knowing that in a few minutes I would have completed by journey home.

I drove straight into the garage, got out of the car and, not stopping to close the doors, I hurried through the back door into the kitchen where John stood preparing the meal. As I passed the cooker, I glanced at the clock. The time was 5.45 pm I said "I'm just going to look out of the bedroom window, then I'll tell you something you won't believe." I rushed up the stairs and looked out of the window to where I had seen the red and green lights. I was expecting to see that strange craft in the sky but by then the clouds were thickening and all I saw was a yellow light flashing approximately where the others had been. Back in the kitchen I again noticed the clock and then realised that I was home later than I would normally expect to be. The journey had taken about fifteen minutes longer than it usually did.

The meal was served, whilst I related the details of my unusual journey home. John didn't say much. I was disappointed. I really did expect him to know all about it. He later described his reaction as 'stunned'. It was certainly in stunned silence that we ate our meal but then I wanted to talk. There were questions to which I needed answers, but he did not have any.

Fascination changed to frustration when suddenly, sometime after seven o'clock, I experienced another tightening sensation around my head exactly as I had done at lunchtime. It also lasted for about a minute then stopped as suddenly as it had started. It was then I remembered the first one.

Why had this happened TWICE today, I wondered? Could they be connected I had been trying to find an explanation for the other strange events that had occurred on that journey home, now here was another to add to them.

I had thought that having arrived safely home that would be the end of it, but now I was wondering if those two identical feelings in my head were related to the journey in some way, and whether the whole experience was one which lasted over a longer period than I had originally supposed. That one at lunchtime could have been the beginning of it all and the one I had just had could (hopefully) have ended it.

There were so many things buzzing around in my head that evening, things which I could not understand. I was not frightened of anything that had happened, but very puzzled indeed.

APPENDIX 2

On the evening of 22nd November 1998 I was going to a Women's Institute Meeting in the village of Preston Capes which is about four miles from the village of Byfield where I lived. I was giving a lift to three ladies who were going to the meeting with me.

We left Byfield village about 7.15 pm then drove to Woodford Halse the next village on our way to Preston Capes. The roads between Byfield and Preston Capes are only narrow country lanes and there are no street lights along them.

Approximately half a mile after leaving Woodford Halse the road climbs a hill with a small wood on the left-hand side. As I approached it and started to drive up it, a beam of white light suddenly shone down into the wood lighting up one of the trees. It was as if a large search light had been switched on and was shining through its branches. Suddenly my car, which was new and had been perfectly all right, started faltering and though I changed down in gear twice the car was still struggling to go. At this point I was worried about the car stopping as we were in a very lonely spot with no telephone. But then I said to my friends, "Where on earth is that light coming from?"

Suddenly as quickly as it had appeared the light went out and the car once again drove perfectly so I continued to the T junction at the top of the hill.

When I stopped at the junction I noticed to my left in the sky there were two stationary lights, a red one on the left and a green one on the right. They appeared to be about a foot apart and at an angle of 45°, which I was later informed meant that these lights were within a quarter of a mile from us. As I looked at these lights they moved across in front of my car to the right-hand side and there they hung stationary. During all this time there was no sound whatsoever. I thought this was very strange as I had travelled along this road many times with jet aircraft passing over head and if there was no sound on one side of you, you could always hear them either pass over head or when they had gone to the other side of you.

During all this I was not frightened, just intrigued. I turned right towards Preston Capes and as I started driving the red and green lights kept pace with my car for about a quarter of a mile. Suddenly the two lights went out and a single brilliant white light came on. Then this light took off at a great speed towards Preston Capes and just disappeared as though it had been switched off.

By now it was approaching 7.30 pm. We carried on to our meeting discussing what we had seen.

A couple of months later when I was again talking through this experience with those same ladies, two of them no longer remembered seeing anything and one just remembered the white light. This seemed so strange to me as I had remembered it all so vividly.

Georgina Laurie

APPENDIX 3

During the evening of 27th September 1990 I had been discussing Healing, Clairvoyance and Clairaudience with a friend and together we had meditated.

As I drove home from Weedon I was thinking everything through when I came to the point where I had driven under my dumb-bell shaped UFO in November 1978.

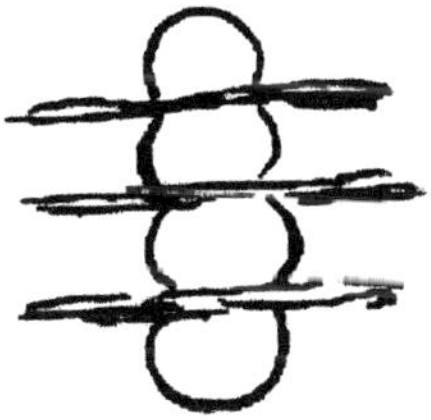

It was 10.15 pm and no stars were visible. Suddenly I became aware of a brightness in the sky to my right and looking in that direction I was able to see what I took to be a fourth moon just forming below a line of three others. Each was below the one above and where each joined there was what appeared to be a narrow strip of cloud crossing in front – a formation of three narrow-like strips of cloud.

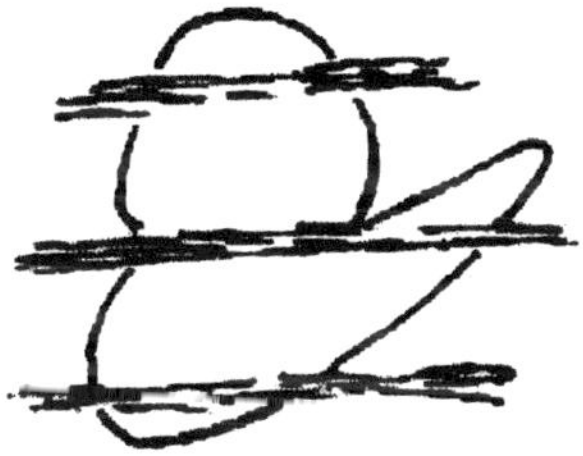

Assuming that there would have been a full moon that night and that it had been reflected against the clouds, I continued to drive along the A5. Then I looked at it again. This time the four 'moons' were squashing downwards and were becoming pear-shaped. There was a brightness in the sky surrounding this and other cloud formation were clearly visible. Then, as I looked, it grew what appeared to be a tail from the bottom out to the right and resembled a small child's drawing of a cat.

At the top of the hill, now off the A5, I could see it again. It was by this time a much larger orangey-yellow ball of light with two tails, one on each side forming the shape of a boomerang – a ball of light sitting on a boomerang.

Continuing my journey I reached the corner of the village where, before, I had found myself sitting in complete darkness and I was again able to observe a further change in shape as I looked between the farm buildings. It was as if it had rolled over and the 'boomerang' was pointing to the right, rather like an arrowhead. I drove on past the Church and there it was again but this time the boomerang-shaped part of the light had disappeared completely. It was just a very large ball about the size of an orange in comparison to the moon which I had estimated would have been about the size of a 2 pence piece. The three narrow strips of cloud were still across it.

In the time it took to drive into the garage and close the garage doors, the whole thing had disappeared. It was 10.20 pm and the sky was completely dark, I could see no moon, stars or clouds. What I had thought to be the moon was no longer there.

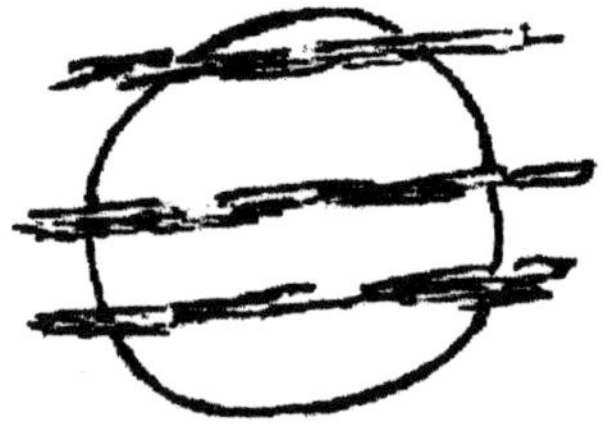

The following night the moon was visible as a half moon but clouds covered that until several days later when the weather changed and when travelling along the same section of road I could see that at the relevant time the almost full moon was high in the sky on the left-hand side of the A5 whilst the 'lights' had been low down on the right-hand side.

APPENDIX 4

THE ANGLER

The angler sat on the river bank
Thinking about his tea.
A fish he spied in the water below,
"Ah!" he said, "that's for me."

He unpacked his rod and fixed on his line.
He opened his tin of bait.
He looked at the flies pinned on his hat.
A decision he had to make.

A maggot or worm? He did not squirm.
He pondered for a while.
Then from his head, to look instead
A fly – and with a satisfied smile

He thought, the worms are good for the garden.
They mix up and aerate the soil.
A pity to harm them when they do so much good.
In the ground they'll be happy to toil.

So the lid on the tin he replaced
With a very satisfied feeling.
Then he picked up the box with the maggots inside
And from it the lid he began peeling.

"You'll only develop into flies," he said,
"Spreading horrendous disease.
You can go the fishes instead
And feed them. Sorry mates – hard cheese!"

So they were flung into the stream
Exciting the fish he could see.
Now, he decided, the next thing to do
Was to take one of them home for his tea.

The fly, he know would help him,
So he attached it with care to his line.
Then he cast it out on to the water –
Well-positioned the very first time.

The ease with which he had done it
Surprised him, to tell you the truth.
Now he must wait and see what happens,
To be furnished with the proof

That he had chosen correctly
The right bait for that kind of fish.
A bell on the end of the line would denote
A completely successful wish.

He lay back in the sunshine
And waited for it to ring.
But of course, by then, he'd fallen asleep
And he never heard a thing.

But he dreamed he had caught a whopper,
So large that it weighed a ton.
But whether he did, we shall never know,
For it got away – that one!